YOUR
MONEY
MATTERS

Author

Your Money Matters:

**Published by Young Money
(part of Young Enterprise)**
Young Enterprise Head Office
Yeoman House
Sekforde St
London
EC1R 0HF

Young Enterprise is a registered charity.
Registered number 313697

© 2018 Young Money

ISBN 978-1-9164672-0-0

Printed in the United Kingdom by Geoff Neal Group.

British Library Cataloguing in Publication Data
A Catalogue record for this publication is available
from the British Library.

Acknowledgments

Young Money would like to take this opportunity
to thank Martin Lewis OBE, Founder of
MoneySavingExpert.com, for his generous donation,
direction and passion that made this project possible.

Young Money would also like to thank the teachers
and consultants who guided the development of
Your Money Matters and the Department
of Education for their help and guidance in the
development of this textbook.

In addition, special thanks to:

Contributing authors
John Chapman
Stewart Jones
Emma Waller
Russell Winnard, Young Money
Liz Booth, Young Money

Other contributors
Robyn Vernon-Harcourt, Young Money
Eileen Gannon, Young Money
Feyi Onamusi, Young Money
Charlotte Churchill, Young Money
Braden Clamp, Young Money

Design by **Something Big Ltd.**
Printed by **Geoff Neal Group**
Proofread by **Melissa Stewart**
Quality Mark by **Young Money**

ENSURE YOU'RE IN THE KNOWS,
NOT IN THE KNOW NOTS.

Foreword by Martin Lewis aka the Money Saving Expert

It's only money isn't it? Well, no, actually. It's far more important than that. I've spent 15 years campaigning on TV and online to get people to be better with their cash. Money isn't just a financial issue, problems can infect every area of your life – your happiness, mental health, work, relationships and more. This isn't intended to scare you, I just don't intend to sugar coat it just because you're still at school.

Of course, you likely already make money choices on a daily basis – such as picking your phone or buying a friend's birthday present – and as you move into independence the decisions grow, whether you dream of getting a car, want to go to Uni, or getting your first job. Throughout all of these, the knowledge and attitudes you have about money will become even more important.

That's what this textbook is about. It's here to start you out on your journey towards financial literacy. While it won't come close to teaching you all the answers you'll need for life, it does cover many of the main ones. Yet even if all you picked up was to take money seriously, to read up and ask questions before big decisions, and gain the skills to do the numbers, it would leave me skipping like a little lamb (not a pleasant image I accept).

While some of your parents and guardians will be great with money – some won't – and it's important we level the playing field. That's one reason I, and many others, campaigned for years to ensure we got financial education on the curriculum. Yet that alone isn't enough. We live in one of the world's most competitive economies, companies spend billions advertising, marketing and teaching their staff to sell, yet we don't get any buyers training.

That needs to change. This textbook aims to make it easier for schools to ensure that every young person receives a high-quality financial education by the time they leave school.

I hope you like it.

Martin Lewis

Young Money is very grateful to Martin Lewis OBE for funding the development and delivery of this textbook into every English state secondary school.

Statement from The Rt Hon Nick Gibb MP:

Economic and financial education are an important part of a broad and balanced curriculum, and provide the essential knowledge that young people need to manage their finances and succeed in the modern world. Both the Department for Education and HM Treasury support high-quality resources for schools to help deliver this, and I would like to commend Martin Lewis and Young Money for making this new textbook available.

Minister of State for School Standards, the Rt Hon Nick Gibb MP

Statement from Michal Mercieca, CEO of Young Money, which is part of the charity Young Enterprise:

It's an increasingly complex world out there for young people, with a huge range of financial decisions that need to be taken from an early age, in the face of ever-increasing technological change in the financial landscape. This textbook aims to help you get to grips with these money choices, which have such an important impact on your future. We couldn't have produced this textbook without Martin Lewis OBE, who funded its development and delivery, and we're extremely grateful for his support. I very much hope that this textbook goes a long way to helping you prepare for your financial future.

Michal Mercieca,
CEO of Young Money,
which is part of the charity
Young Enterprise

YOUR MONEY
MATTERS

About Young Money

Young Money (formerly pfeg), supports all educators in developing the financial capability of the young people they work with. We are a trusted and valued provider of knowledge, resources and training to anyone teaching children and young people how to manage money.

We offer schools free resources and support to make teaching financial education easy. We know that every school and college is unique and needs to find its' own solution to meeting the needs of its' learners.

We believe that trained teachers provide the most effective and sustainable route for financial education in schools as they know their pupils best and understand how to integrate financial education into lessons and meet the requirements of their school curriculum.

Please visit us at www.young-money.org.uk to get ideas, inspiration, advice and to access our full range of resources and services.

Contact

Young Enterprise Head Office
Yeoman House
Sekforde St
London
EC1R 0HF

T. 020 7330 9470
E. info@y-m.org.uk

Follow us on twitter @YoungMoneyEdu

Young Enterprise is a registered charity. Registered number 313697
Incorporated in England as a Company Limited by Guarantee No. 712260

YOUR MONEY MATTERS
CONTENTS

HOW TO USE
THIS TEXTBOOK

Welcome to Your Money Matters. This book will help you make informed choice about managing your money, now and in the future.

There are six chapters on topics that are relevant to you. Each starts with a question, which the information included in the chapter will help you answer.

In each chapter, you will find:

INFORMATION
The information icon highlights key and useful information on the chapter topic.

DID YOU KNOW?
Look out for the these icons, which will give interesting facts on the subject area.

ACTIVITY
The pencil icon indicates there is an activity for you to complete to help build your knowledge and understanding of the information you have read.

DISCUSSION
The discussions provide an opportunity for to you talk to your classmates about the topic areas and give your opinion on key information within the chapter.

CASE STUDY
The case studies let you examine real-life situations in more detail and decide what you think the best course of action is.

QUESTIONS
You will find questions at the end of each section. The questions are an opportunity for you to apply the knowledge you have gained through reading the information and check your understanding.

WHAT HAVE YOU LEARNT?
Each chapter reviews learning with a 'What have you learnt?' section, which include summary activities and case studies for you to complete, drawing on the knowledge you have gained throughout the chapter.

FURTHER YOUR KNOWLEDGE
At the end of each chapter, there is an additional section which includes further and more detailed information about the subject area, and extension activities to stretch your learning.

YOUR
MONEY
MATTERS

SAVING
IS IT IMPORTANT FOR ME
TO SAVE MY MONEY?

In this chapter you will explore the reasons that people save money, and how to compare the range of saving options available.

You'll see how saving is an important way of reaching future financial goals, and how individual choice is important in making those decisions.

By the end of the chapter, you will know what your main options are for saving your money and be able to make comparisons between them. You'll be aware of some of the main features and perks that can come with savings options, and how to take these into account in your decision making.

DID YOU KNOW?

There are over 300 banks and 45 building societies registered in the UK. All provide a wide range of savings options for customers.

UNIVERSITY
HOUSE
WEDDING

HOLIDAY
CAR
MOBILE PHONE

SAVINGS

SAVING OR SAVINGS?

It is easy to confuse the terms saving and savings.

Saving is often thought of as the act of putting away money for future use. This might range from a few pence being kept in a money box at home to a larger amount being placed in a bank account.

Saving can also refer to reducing the amount you spend, maybe allowing you to put some of that money away for future use.

Savings refers to the amount or value of the money that is being put to one side. If you have put £50 into a bank account this is your savings. If you then arrange to put in a further £10 per month then that is the amount you are saving. In this example, at the end of 1 year you would have saved a further £120 (£10 x 12 months) on top of the initial £50, giving you a total savings amount of £170 altogether. This is the amount that is said to have accrued.

Reasons to save:

- For a very specific purpose or to help achieve a particular goal
- To gather together wealth for future use
- To put money aside for unplanned events
- To keep your money safe.

DISCUSSION

Think about the different reasons people might have for saving money. Come up with two examples for each of the reasons above.

DELAYED GRATIFICATION

When you save money, it is likely that you will spend it at some point in the future. That could be either in the next few days or weeks (short-term saving) or within the next year (medium-term saving). It may even be much further into the future (long-term saving) – for example, when you are saving up for somewhere to live or even thinking about retirement. In some cases, the money you save may be passed on to others through gifts, donations to charity or inheritance.

Saving for future spending is sometimes called "delayed gratification" – in other words, we postpone the sense of enjoyment we get from immediate spending to sometime further into the future. But remember, the money can only be spent once, so the choices you make about how to spend your savings should be made very carefully.

Saving can bring its own sense of satisfaction – if you're saving on a regular basis and can see your savings increase as you move towards your target amount.

ACTIVITY

1. Sam currently spends all of his £5 pocket money every week on a music streaming subscription. There is currently an offer to make a one-off payment of £80 for a whole year of streaming.

a) How many weeks will it take Sam to save up the money for the one-off payment?

b) How much would Sam save over the year?

c) Do you think it is worth the wait to save up for the one-off payment?

d) What might the disadvantages be?

2. Jakob has saved up for a new game to play on his console. He can buy it online now for £40, plus £5 postage and packaging, or he can wait 3 months, save a bit more and buy the downloadable version, which will have added features and levels, for £55. He can only spend the money that he's saved up once, so needs to decide what to do.

a) Identify the benefits and implications of each option.

b) In your opinion, should Jakob delay buying the game? What would you do?

QUESTIONS

1. What is the difference between 'saving' and 'savings'?

2. Identify three benefits of someone having savings.

3. What might be the consequences of not having savings?

4. Give an example of delayed gratification.

WAYS TO SAVE

The simplest way to save is to put some cash to one side at home. This is usually fine for small amounts but becomes increasingly risky as the amount of savings becomes larger. Cash in the home is at risk of being stolen or lost, and it can be difficult to keep track of exactly how much you have in order to know if any is missing. That's why many people choose to keep their money in a safer place such as a bank, building society or credit union.

DID YOU KNOW?

Banks, building societies and credit unions are all organisations that provide financial services, including the ability to save, but are structured differently.

A bank is an organisation owned by its shareholders. It aims to maximise profits for its shareholders through its financial activities.

A building society is an organisation that is owned by its members, some of whom will be customers who save money with or borrow money from the society. They often offer a range of financial services and are similar to banks.

Credit unions are community focused, non-profit making organisations that encourage saving and lend money to members. To use a credit union, you have to become a member.

TYPES OF ACCOUNT

There are two main types of account which can be opened at a bank, building society or credit union:

- **Current accounts.** These help you to manage your day-to-day money, pay bills, receive incoming money and help keep your money secure. Most standard current accounts are free to use.

  Many banks and building societies offer current accounts with extra incentives, for example: holiday or mobile phone insurance, cheaper rates on loans and mortgages, and money off holidays and flights. These have a monthly fee of between £10 and £20 and are called "packaged accounts". However, you should only consider one of these current accounts if you know that the annual cost of the package is less than if you were to buy the incentives separately.

  There is also a switching service available that allows you to move your current account from one bank or building society to another. They may provide you with vouchers, cash and better interest rates as a reward to switch to them.

  Some current accounts pay interest on the money you have in them and may even pay more than a savings account (although this is often only up to a limit of around £3,000).

- **Savings accounts.** These are specifically designed for you to save money in and are usually best for saving larger amounts. The amount you put in may grow as interest is added. Interest is an extra payment given as a reward for keeping your money with that particular organisation. They may also be referred to as deposit accounts.

We'll look in more detail at the different types of savings account later in this chapter.

DID YOU KNOW?

All UK-regulated current or savings accounts and cash ISAs (Individual Savings Accounts) in banks, building societies and credit unions are covered by the Financial Services Compensation Scheme (FSCS).

This means that if they fail you would get back up to £85,000 per person, per financial institution.

QUESTIONS

1. Give three advantages of keeping money in a bank account rather than at home.
2. What is the difference between a current account and a savings account?
3. How do you think someone might use a current account and a savings account together?
4. Some people have more than one savings account. Why might this be the case?

INTEREST

A REWARD FOR SAVING

As well as being a safer option for storing savings, people choose to save with a bank or building society because they offer interest on money saved with them. Interest is the reward you get for keeping your money with a bank or a building society. It is also the cost you pay when you borrow money through a loan or credit agreement – see the 'Borrowing' chapter. It is usually worked out as a percentage, known as the interest rate. From this, you can work out how much interest is going to be earned on top of the money you save.

There are two ways of working out interest – simple interest and compound interest. In reality, all banks will use the compound method to work out the interest they pay or charge you, but let's look at the simple interest method first to see why this is:

The interest earned on an initial amount of £1,000 (known as the **P**rincipal) deposited into a savings account with an interest rate of 2%, or 0.02 in decimal format (known as the **R**ate), for 1 year (known as the **T**ime) can be worked out using the simple interest formula:

Interest = P x R x T

In this case, this would be, 1000 x 0.02 x 1.

So, an interest rate of 2% paid on a principal of £1,000 would gain £20 interest over 1 year. This will only be accurate if no further money, on top of the original £1,000, is deposited or withdrawn.

This method of calculating interest is known as the simple interest method. It suggests that the principal amount would earn £20 every year.

ACTIVITY

1. Using the simple interest formula, calculate the interest if the £1,000 were kept in the savings account at the same interest rate of 2% for:

a) 3 years **b)** 7 years **c)** 15 years

(HINT – use the formula but change **T** to the different number of years the money is saved.)

2. Can you see anything slightly unfair with the calculations you have made in Q1?

(HINT – think about the amount you are receiving interest on each year.)

COMPOUND INTEREST

In reality, organisations use a different method of calculating interest known as compound interest. This recognises that at the end of year 1, your total savings would be £1,020 and that in year 2 you should have your interest calculated against this higher amount. This means that the interest gained in previous years will also earn interest – meaning you receive a higher return on top of your savings.

Interest on interest on interest...

So, if the £1,000 is deposited for 3 years and the 2% rate is compounded it will work out as follows:

Year 1: £1,000 x 0.02 x 1 = £20.00 interest. Total savings at the end of Year 1 = £1,020

Year 2: £1,020 x 0.02 x 1 = £20.40 interest. Total savings at the end of Year 2 = £1,040.40

Year 3: £1,040.40 x 0.02 x 1 = 20.81 interest. Total savings at the end of Year 3 = **£1,061.21**

So, over 3 years with a principal sum of £1,000 you would receive £1.21 more if the interest was calculated using the compound method compared to the simple interest method. Not a huge difference? Well, that's true on smaller amounts saved over short time periods but, for larger amounts over longer time periods, the interest gained will be much more significant.

This method of calculating compound interest is really good to use when there are only a small number of years to calculate but imagine if you had savings of 10 years or more...it would take you much longer to work out the answer. Therefore, another way of calculating compound interest is using the multiplier, for example if £50,000 was saved over 15 years at an interest rate of 2% the total value of savings would be:

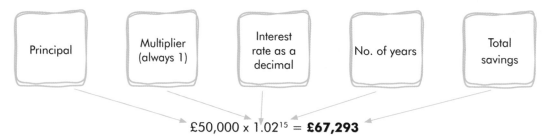

$$£50,000 \times 1.02^{15} = \textbf{£67,293}$$

So, the amount of interest earned over 15 years would be

$$£67,293 - £50,000 = \textbf{£17,297}$$

If we had used the simple interest method, the total interest would have been:

£50,000 x 0.02 x 15 = **£15,000**, so the total value of the savings would have been **£65,000**.

In this scenario, using the compound method would mean you would receive £2,293 more interest. That's £2,293 more, just because of the way the interest is calculated.

This final amount will only be reached if no further money is deposited or withdrawn. In reality, more money may have been added to the amount being saved or some of it taken out to be spent. Therefore, the amount actually being saved will vary constantly; this will in turn affect the amount of interest being accrued.

DID YOU KNOW?

The formula for compound interest, which you will use in GCSE Maths, is:

$$\text{Total accrued} = P \left(1 + \frac{r}{100}\right)^n$$

ACTIVITY

The chart below shows the average annual savings interest rates in the UK from 1990 to 2017.

1. Summarise what has happened to savings interest rates over this 27 year period.

2. If you had put £1,000 into a savings account in 1990, how much interest would you have earned over the year?

3. If you had put £1,000 into a savings account in 2017, how much interest would you have earned over the year?

4. Look at your answers for Q2 and Q3, what does this tell us about interest rates?

5. Look at the trend over the 27 years, what would you say is likely to happen to savings interest rates in the future?

ACTIVITY

1. Use the compound method to calculate the interest paid on a principal of £150,000 saved in a savings account paying 3% interest over the following periods:

a) 5 years **b)** 12 years **c)** 20 years

2. What if the interest rate was 5%? Use the same information in Q1 to recalculate the interest received.

3. Calculate Q1 and Q2 using the simple interest method and compare the difference in interest received to the compound method.

Annual average UK interest savings rates

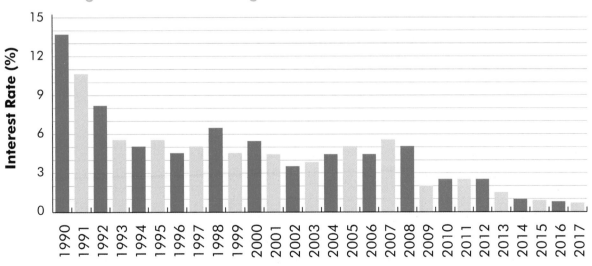

DID YOU KNOW?

Banks tend to calculate the interest on your savings on a daily basis using the compound method, although the period that they pay the interest to you can vary from one savings account to another.

Take a look at the following table, which shows what would happen if banks were to calculate the interest payable on £5,000 at a rate of 3% for 5 years over different compounding periods.

SIMPLE INTEREST	COMPOUND INTEREST			
	Yearly	Quarterly	Monthly	Daily
£5,750	£5,796.37	£5,805.92	£5,808.08	£5,809.14

DISCUSSION

Why do you think banks calculate interest on a daily basis?

Why do you think different institutions pay interest out at different intervals?

ACTIVITY

1. ZYX Bank offers a saver rate of 1.5% and a borrowing rate of 9.5% per year. Calculate the profit the bank would make if an amount of £2,000 was saved and then lent out over 1 year.

2. Explain what would happen if the borrowing interest rate was lower than the saving interest rate.

DID YOU KNOW?

It is important to remember that interest on savings are a form of income and are subject to tax (except ISAs - we will look at these later on). There are limits as to how much interest you can earn before it becomes taxed. These are set out in the Personal Savings Allowance (PSA), but for most people they would have to earn over £1,000 interest a year before paying any tax.

WHY DO BANKS PAY INTEREST?

Banks pay interest as a way of attracting people to save with them. While they have your money, they are able to make use of it, for example, it can be lent to borrowers. When a bank lends money to borrowers it will do so at a higher interest rate than it pays to its savers.

This is why it is better to save than borrow, because in effect you get paid to save whereas you have to pay to borrow.

If you have borrowed money from a bank, you should try to pay this off before you start saving. This is because it costs you more to borrow than save.

For example, ABC Bank pays savers an interest rate of 2% a year, but charges borrowers an interest rate of 10% a year. If a saver put £1,000 into their savings account for a year ABC Bank would pay them £20 interest.

Over that same period, if ABC Bank loaned the £1,000 to a borrower the bank would receive £100 in interest at the end of the year.

In total, ABC Bank have made £80 profit. This would be £100 interest from the borrower minus £20 interest they have paid to the saver. This is how banks and other financial institutions make some of their profits.

COMPARING INTEREST RATES AND THE ROLE OF ANNUAL EQUIVALENT RATE (AER)?

You might think it would be really easy to compare two savings accounts by looking at the interest rates they offer. Well, it's actually not always as easy as you might think.

Some savings accounts have charges associated with them, for example, when withdrawing cash at short notice. While some savings accounts offer additional perks and bonuses, for example, a higher interest rate for the first year.

To make comparing the interest on savings account easier it is shown as an Annual Equivalent Rate (AER). This takes into account the charges and the interest paid on the account and shows it as an overall percentage rate. This means that savers can easily compare savings accounts from different banks. The higher the AER the more interest they will receive on their savings.

QUESTIONS

1. Why do financial organisations offering similar savings products have different interest rates?

2. Why is the Annual Equivalent Rate (AER) used to work out overall interest on a savings account?

3. Explain the advantage of compound interest compared to simple interest.

4. Which is better for a saver – an account which calculates interest daily, monthly or yearly?

5. AER is one way to compare savings accounts, but what else should you consider when choosing the right account for you?

THE IMPACT OF INFLATION

Inflation is simply the general increase in the cost of goods and services from one year to the next. The government calculates this figure every month and publishes it as a percentage. The higher the inflation rate, the greater the increase in cost of everyday goods and services.

For example, if the inflation rate was 2% then a weekly food shop that cost you £100 last year would be expected to cost £102 this year.

If the rate of inflation is higher than the interest rate on savings, it means that the cost of goods and services are increasing faster than the level of interest received. Therefore, the amount you can purchase with the savings will have reduced.

So, if you have savings, or if you're looking for a new savings account, make sure to keep an eye on how the interest rate you will be receiving compares to the rate of inflation.

DID YOU KNOW?

The interest rate you get on your savings is influenced by the Bank of England. They set a base rate, which banks then use to help set the interest rate they offer on their savings accounts.

The Bank of England have an opportunity to change this rate eight times per year, however, unless they have made an explicit promise not to do so, high street banks can vary their interest rates whenever they want.

If you want to learn more about how savings can work for you then go to

www.moneysavingexpert.com/savings

SAVINGS ACCOUNT FEATURES

While the AER gives a very good indication of the amount of interest you will receive on your savings, it's not the only thing to look for in a savings account. There are different types of savings accounts with features that appeal to different people:

TYPE OF SAVINGS ACCOUNT	DEFINITION	ACCOUNT FEATURES
Easy access accounts	This type of account allows you to withdraw money at any time without prior warning. Often these are "instant access" accounts, which allow you to withdraw any amount of money from an ATM straight away for free.	• May offer a higher interest rate when first set up • Interest rate tends to be lower than for other accounts • May be restrictions on how many withdrawals you can make every year, so make sure you check the small print
Notice account	Advance warning usually has to be given if you wish to withdraw money from this type of account without being penalised.	• Typically, 30, 60 or 90 days advance notice has to be given to withdraw money • Withdrawing money without giving notice could result in loss of interest • Generally have a better interest rate as the bank knows when you will be taking money out, and can plan accordingly
Regular saver account	A regular sum of money must be added to the account each month.	• The interest rate is usually higher • The number of withdrawals that can be made from the account may be limited • In all cases, there is a limit to how much you can save (usually around £250 per month)
Fixed rate savings (sometimes called bonds)	Your saved money is "locked away" for a specified period of time (known as the term). A bond is another word for a loan. This means that you are lending your money to a bank or building society in return for interest.	• A one-off amount often must be deposited at the start • The term is usually between 1 and 5 years • A fixed (and usually higher) interest rate is offered – depending on how much money is deposited and how long the term is • You may be able to withdraw money before the term is up, but this will usually result in penalties, which are often higher than for a Notice account
Individual Savings Account (ISA)	This is a form of savings account where you do not pay tax on the interest earned.	• The government set the limit of how much money you can save in an ISA each tax year

These different forms of savings account are available from a wide range of banks and building societies, although the interest rate you receive will vary from one organisation to another. That means that while a higher rate of interest might be expected on a regular savings account, or fixed interest account, there could still be better rates to be found on easy access accounts. The golden rule is to always look around!

All of the above forms of savings account can be taken out as an ISA. This means that you are not taxed on the interest you receive up to a certain limit, which the government set each year. More details about ISAs can be found later on in the chapter.

PREMIUM BONDS

Premium bonds are a form of savings account offered by the government backed savings bank – National Savings and Investment (NS&I). You can buy premium bonds by paying between £100 and £50,000 to the NS&I. However, rather than receiving interest on the amount you save, every £1 saved comes with a unique bond number, which is entered into a monthly prize draw for the chance to win a cash prize of between £25 and £1,000,000 tax free. So, if you saved £500 you would have 500 bond numbers entered in the draw each month.

CHOOSING WHAT'S RIGHT FOR YOU

It's very easy to just look at the interest rate when choosing a savings account and pick the one with the highest rate, but that may not always be the best option for you. Think about how often you'll need access to your savings, whether you can make regular payments in or not, whether you need online or telephone banking, and what the minimum opening requirements are. It may well be that the savings account that works best for you is not always the one which offers the highest interest.

DID YOU KNOW?

The odds of each £1 bond number winning a prize is 24,500 to 1.

ACTIVITY

The following young people are all looking to set up a savings account.

GENE
16 YEARS OLD

Gene gets a monthly allowance from his parents but spends all of this on his everyday costs. He also has a Saturday job in a sports store working for 6 hours at a rate of £4.50 per hour.

He is using the money he earns from his Saturday job to save up for a new bike which costs £750, but he can get a 10% staff discount on this.

So far, he has saved £300, but he keeps it in a box in his wardrobe and he's not sure it's safe, so he's looking to open a bank account.

NANDITA
17 YEARS OLD

Nandita has a Saturday job, working in her aunt's restaurant. She works for five hours and earns £4.25 per hour and averages an extra £10 each Saturday in tips, but by mid-week there's never much left.

Nandita's aunt wants her to open a bank account so that she can pay her wages directly into an account.

Nandita would love to go on holiday with her friends in 6 months' time – her parents have volunteered to pay for the holiday, but she'll still want to take spending money.

ADI
15 YEARS OLD

Adi manages his money carefully. He gets a weekly allowance of £12 and prefers to receive monetary gifts for birthdays, etc.

Although he's not saving for anything specific, he knows that having some money put away for when he needs it is a good thing. He tends to think decisions about purchases through carefully, rather than making snap decisions (apart from downloading music).

He thinks he'll probably go to university in a few years' time, but until then he needs a bank account that will suit his current needs.

Have a look at the four different savings account options below and choose the most appropriate account for each individual, giving at least two reasons for your decision.

PLUSH ACCOUNT	JUNIOR PLUSH ACCOUNT	PLUSH ONE ACCOUNT	SUPER PLUSH ACCOUNT
• 0.5% AER • Open an account with just £5 and receive a free gift • ATM card (age 16+) • Online and telephone banking (age 16+) • Monthly paper statements (with the option to go paperless)	• 2% AER • ATM card • £10 minimum to open an account • Age range: 14-18 years • £25 gift card when you open an account	• 2.25% AER • £75 minimum to open account • 30 days' notice to withdraw money without loss of interest • Minimum age to open account: 16 • Internet banking only	• 2.75 % AER • ATM card • £100 minimum to open • Monthly deposit of £50 required • No notice required for withdrawals (up to a limit of £200)

QUESTIONS

1. Why might someone choose to open an account where they have to give a period of notice before withdrawing savings?

2. What is the main benefit of an ISA?

3. Give an example of when you might use a fixed rate savings bond.

4. Come up with five things you should consider before choosing which savings account is right for you. Explain why you should consider each of these.

HOW TO GET THE MONEY
TO SAVE

Putting your money into a savings account is a safe and largely risk-free way to save for the future. However, getting the money to be able to save in the first place can be a challenge. There are four main ways in which you can get money to save:

Earn it

Increasing earnings, through extra work or an increase in pay, may enable you to save more of your income. When you get an increase in earnings the extra income can very easily become part of your everyday spending, so a good trick is to put the extra bit of income into your savings straight away – that way you don't feel as if you're missing out!

Be given it

There are many occasions in life when you may be given money – for a birthday, as a gift, or even as an inheritance.

Sell things you own

It is now easier than ever before to sell your belongings. For example, you might have games consoles, mobile phones or even clothing, which you no longer use. These may have value to others and make you some extra money in the process.

Reduce your spending

Reviewing your spending and making more informed spending choices can have a serious impact on the amount of money you have left to save.

TOP TIPS

Here are just a few ways you could reduce your spending:

 1. Price check everything using comparison sites – find out which retailer is selling your favourite computer games or latest gadget the cheapest.

 2. Use discount vouchers or money-off coupons – you can easily find these online, in magazines and newspapers, or in shops.

 3. Join online cashback sites – if you buy online, sign up to a cashback site and every time you use that shop, you will get a certain percentage of money back for using the site.

 4. Follow your favourite shops on social media – you will find out when they are having sales or clearing old stock.

 5. Declutter your bank account – cancel unused gym memberships, monthly subscriptions and change your phone contract to a cheaper one if you can.

DID YOU KNOW?

According to The Money Advice Service, 4 in 10 working age people have less than £100 saved in total.

 6. Always ask yourself, "Do I really need it?"

 7. Walk or cycle, rather than pay for taxis or train and bus fares – it's better for your wallet and your heart.

 8. Make a savings plan or use a savings app to help you save for the short or long term.

Once you start to pay your own bills, take the time to do your research to find the best money-saving deals.

Can you think of any other ways to save? Do some research of your own and think about ways that suit you.

 ACTIVITY

Think about some of the expensive items and events that you may have to save for in the future, then:

1. List five items and/or events that you may have to save for as an adult.

2. Estimate how much you think these may cost you.

3. Consider different ways you could save up for these.

4. Consider what obstacles may stand in your way of saving for these items/events.

5. Decide how you may overcome these obstacles.

6. Are you surprised about any of your answers? How does this make you feel?

 ## CASE STUDY

Using your knowledge about saving, read the following scenarios and suggest how each person could save. Also consider the implications if they choose not to save.

1. Wasim has just started sixth form college and wants the latest designer trainers. His mum has told him that he already has a wardrobe full of trainers and that if he wants them, he must save the money himself.

2. Chloe is 18 and plans to go to university this year. She will be living independently, away from home. She currently has a part time job earning about £100 per week. She wants to save about £1,000 for emergency funds, just in case.

3. Ayomide has completed an apprenticeship in IT and starts his new job next month. To celebrate, he wants to go on holiday with his friends. He has a credit card and has decided to use this to pay for the trip and his spending money – he will worry about the bill when he gets back! He has some savings but if he uses these it will leave his bank account empty.

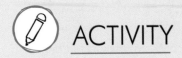 ACTIVITY

Wasim decides to put together a savings plan so that he can get his new trainers.

- He needs £70

- It will take him 3 months

His savings plan is shown below:

DATE	I PLAN TO SAVE (£)	HOW WILL I SAVE THIS?	I STILL NEED TO SAVE (£)
January	£10	Pocket money I get from Nan	£60
February	£30	Birthday money	£30
February	£10	Pocket money I get from Nan	£20
March	£20	Chores around the house – washing car, cleaning room and taking dog for a walk	£0

Wasim reaches his goal of saving £70, but in the meantime he has turned 17 and now wants to start driving lessons instead of buying the trainers. Booking a set of lessons will cost him £140, so he needs to save more money on top of what he has already got. He anticipates that his income will be:

- £10 per month pocket money from his Nan.

- He usually gets the bus to college, but from April he intends to walk rather than get the bus, reducing his expenditure by £15 per month which he can keep.

- Sell an old pair of his trainers for £10 on a popular online selling site in May.

1. Update and complete Wasim's savings plan.

2. In what month will Wasim be able to pay for his driving lessons?

3. What obstacles may stand in the way of his savings plan?

4. What other savings options does Wasim have?

MONEY AND MENTAL HEALTH

Saving is good for our mental health. If we know that we have some savings to cover an unexpected bill, for example, fixing the car or replacing a broken boiler, then it means that we do not have to worry about how we are going to afford to pay for it. Having savings may also mean that we do not need to borrow money and pay for credit. This can reduce stress and gives people more independence over their spending.

 ## CASE STUDY

Abby and Paul both work and have just about enough money each month to pay the bills. However, when birthdays come around they often have to rely on their bank overdraft to pay for the gifts. They are always worrying about what will happen if the washing machine breaks down and not being able to pay for their children's school trips. They have been asked to go on holiday with some family friends and have agreed to go, despite having no savings. Abby only really said yes because she doesn't want her friends to think that she is skint. Paul is upset that Abby has agreed to this and this has put some strain on their relationship.

In groups, discuss the following questions:

1. What impact could this situation have on Abby and Paul's mental health?

2. What effects has not saving had on Abby and Paul?

3. What savings advice would you give to Abby and Paul?

WHAT HAVE YOU LEARNT?

Using the knowledge you have gained from this chapter, can you help Sofia to manage her money better?

Sofia has never been very good at managing her money and previously got into debt by not being careful with her spending. However, she has been saving her £2 coins in a jar recently and she has managed to save a total of £136. She would like to save another £32 within the next month to reach her savings goal so that she can buy some new headphones.

1. Discuss the reasons why leaving the money in a jar may not be the best place to store her savings.

2. Give Sofia some advice about the savings account options that are available to her. Explain why you think these accounts are appropriate for Sofia.

3. Discuss other ways that Sofia could save the remaining £32.

4. Sofia really wants to get new headphones straight away and is desperate to buy some now. She knows that if she buys cheaper ones, they will not be as good as the ones that she wants. What should she do?

5. Sofia still owes £40 on her credit card. Should she pay this off or buy the headphones? Explain your answer.

6. Recommend how Sofia could manage her spending more carefully in future.

7. If Sofia continues to get into debt, how may this affect her mental health?

FURTHER
YOUR KNOWLEDGE

COMPOUNDING INTEREST OVER DIFFERENT PERIODS

Compound interest can be calculated yearly, quarterly (every three months), monthly, weekly or even daily. At the end of each time period the interest accrued is added to the account. In the next time period, interest is earned on the new total (original amount plus the interest added). So, the amount of interest earned increases from one period to the next. In theory, the more often the compounding then the better the return (all other factors being equal).

For example, if £5,000 is placed into a savings account for 10 years and the interest rate is 5% and compounded monthly, then the formula for calculating the value of the savings would be:

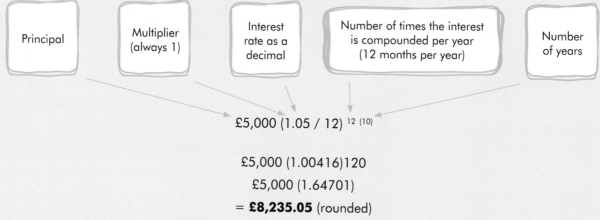

$$£5,000 (1.05 / 12)^{12 (10)}$$

$$£5,000 (1.00416)120$$
$$£5,000 (1.64701)$$
$$= £8,235.05 \text{ (rounded)}$$

So the amount of interest earned over 10 years would be:

$$£8,235.05 - £5,000 = £3,235.05$$

Work out how much interest will have accrued in the following savings accounts:

	PRINCIPAL DEPOSITED	INTEREST RATE	COMPOUND PERIOD	NUMBER OF YEARS
A	£3,000	2.5%	Quarterly	6
B	£6,500	3.25%	Weekly	4
C	£8,325	2.76%	Daily	7

By rearranging the formula, you can solve other variables too. For instance, you can find out what interest rate you need to seek to reach a particular savings goal. You can also see what difference it makes when various compounding periods are used.

PERSONAL SAVINGS ALLOWANCE

As you have discovered, savings generate interest; this is classified as a form of income, and income can be taxed. The Personal Savings Allowance (PSA) was introduced in April 2016 and allows savers to earn a certain amount of interest before tax has to be paid on it.

A basic rate taxpayer (20% tax on income) can earn £1,000 interest on savings per tax year without paying tax on it.

Higher rate taxpayers (who move into the 40% tax bracket) can earn £500 interest on their savings before being taxed.

Additional rate taxpayers (whose income extends into the 45% tax bracket) get no allowance.

It is estimated that only 5% of people will ever pay tax on the interest generated by their savings.

For more information on income tax allowances, see the 'Moving on from school – the world of work' chapter.

If the money saved is held in a joint account, then for purposes of the allowance the interest is regarded as being equally split between the named account holders. The PSA is in addition to an ISA allowance.

In the following examples, calculate the amount of tax payable on savings interest after a year – if any:

1. Zane has already saved £2,000 in a bank account paying 1.55% interest. He now regularly adds £50 per month to this savings account. He is a basic rate tax payer.

2. After a windfall, Camila has locked away total savings of £60,000 earning 2.2% interest paid. She is a basic rate taxpayer.

3. Ali is a higher rate tax payer with three personal savings accounts. At the end of the year he has the following amounts in them:

   - Account A: £35,000 earning annual interest at 1.5%

   - Account B: £10,000 earning annual interest at 1.0%

   - Account C: £500 earning annual interest at 0.8%

4. Ava and Will are a married couple and have a joint savings account. This has £38,000 in it, earning interest at a rate of 1.7% annually. They also have separate savings accounts with £25,000 (1.3% interest rate) and £17,000 (1.6% interest rate) in them respectively. They both have ISAs of £15,000 each (1.2% interest rate). Ava pays tax at the higher rate while Will is on the basic rate.

DISCUSSION

Is it fair that additional rate taxpayers get no PSA?

ISAS

An ISA (Individual Savings Account) is a way of saving or investing money which means tax does not have to be paid on any gains (interest on savings, or income and increases in value of investments). The two main types of ISA are a Cash ISA and a Stocks and Shares ISA. The 2018/19 limit on the amount which can be saved per year is £20,000; this amount is reviewed annually by the government. Interest paid out on cash ISAs does not count towards a Personal Savings Allowance (PSA).

	CASH ISA	STOCKS AND SHARES ISA
	Saving without paying tax on the interest.	Investing in a range of shares, bonds and funds without paying tax on any gains.
Suitability	For short, medium and long term saving by most types of saver.	Most suitable for investment schemes of at least 5 years and only for those who accept they may not get back the full amount invested.
Risk	No risk. The amount of the money saved will stay the same or possibly increase.	Some risk. The value of the money invested may rise or fall in line with the stock market, so it's possible to get back less than the amount invested.
Return	Returns are limited by the stated interest rate.	Unlimited returns possible (but see above).
Age limits	Must be 16 years or over.	Must be 18 years or over.

Although these are the main types of ISA there are others, for example: Junior ISA – a long term, tax free savings account for children under 18, which becomes a normal ISA when they turn 18; and Lifetime ISA – a long term, tax free savings account that is often used for first time property buyers or to build savings for when you retire. The UK government also contributes towards these savings.

 ## ACTIVITY

Carry out some research and find out about the other types of ISAs. Then create a detailed fact sheet entitled "ISAs for Beginners", which compares and contrasts the key aspects of different ISA products. Include a section which looks at how interest accrues over time and another that examines potential benefits and/or risks.

MAKING THE MOST OF YOUR MONEY

HOW DO I MAKE SURE I GET THE MOST FROM MY MONEY?

We all make choices with money nearly every day – whether to spend it or not, what to spend it on, and searching for the best deals.

This chapter looks at some of the things that can influence these choices, how we can manage those choices more effectively and what our consumer rights are for the things we do spend money on.

 DID YOU KNOW?

With a debit card you are spending your own money from your bank account; with a credit card you are spending someone else's, and it must be repaid.

SPENDING

 ## NEEDS AND WANTS

We all spend money, but what we spend it on varies from one person to another. Spending can be split into needs and wants:

- **Needs** – These are the absolute necessities; the things you really cannot do without. Some of these are obvious, such as water, food or housing, although you may still need to make choices about them, such as which brands to buy, which will impact on the price.

- **Wants** – These are the items, services or experiences you would like to buy if you have the money to do so. This is where personal choice and preferences really come into focus. It is all a matter of the priority placed on each of these by each individual.

 ## DISCUSSION

Would you rate a smartphone as a need or a want? Discuss with others and share your views. Does your view change depending on:

- The age of the individual?

- Where in the world they live?

- The amount of money they have?

INFLUENCES ON SPENDING

It's not always just our own needs and wants that determine how we spend our money. We can be influenced in a whole range of ways:

- **Family** – We often learn our money habits from our parents, older siblings and other family members. What they buy tends to influence what we buy, and how they use their money tends to affect the way we use it as well.

- **Peers** – Most of us want to be accepted by our friends and so we buy what they buy to be a part of the group. Social media has had a huge role to play in this in recent years. For example, following celebrities on social media platforms can influence how we spend our money. We may like the products and services that they endorse and want the same, despite the cost.

- **Culture** – Our cultural and religious background means we may develop a particular view of money and how it is spent.

- **Seasonal** – National events such as Christmas, Eid and Rosh Hashanah promote the idea of spending money on certain things at certain times of the year.

- **Advertising** – It is the job of any business to sell us their products. There is a huge advertising industry which helps to create wants in our minds. A good example of this is buying new clothes to follow fashion trends. We may not actually need another pair of trainers but may buy them because we want them or feel we need them, and this is often due to advertising campaigns.

- **Disposable income** – This is the amount of money that we have left at the end of each month once all of the bills have been paid. For example, the more disposable income you have, the more likely you might be to buy things you don't really need just because you have the money available to spend.

It is really useful to be aware of what influences your own spending. If you know what the influencers are, you have a good chance of managing them!

Do your research

Making sure you are aware of the choices you have is also really important when it comes to making spending decisions. Doing research can make a big difference; it can help with:

- Identifying exactly what it is you need

- The range of prices that exist for the same product – the same product can be priced differently from one supplier or retailer to another

- Finding out what others thought of the product and whether it was value for money – product reviews are often available online

- Whether there will be any newer versions of the product coming soon – technology products, such as mobile phones, can change very quickly.

DISCUSSION

Which three influences do you think are the most likely to affect individual decisions at the following ages?

- 7 years old

- 14 years old

- 25 years old

ACTIVITY

Read the following social media profiles for people in different age brackets.

1. For each person identify what you think the top three influences on their spending might be. Give reasons for your answers.

2. Who is likely to have the most and the least disposable income? How might this affect their spending?

3. Who is likely to be influenced the most by social media? How will this affect their spending?

4. Advertisers spend a lot of time and money understanding what influences the spending of customers. In your opinion, do you believe this is money well spent? Give reasons for your answer.

JENAYA

About me

Gender: Female
Age: 16
Location: Yorkshire
Hometown: Leeds
Employment: Student – just started A levels

Activities and Interests

Reading, football, cooking (especially baking), Vlogging, my pet cat Oscar

Music
James Bay, Taylor Swift, Ariana Grande

Books
Harry Potter series, The Hunger Games, anything by John Green

Movies
The Fault in Our Stars, Wonder Woman, Star Wars

Television
Match of the Day, The Simpsons, The Great British Bake Off

SIMON

About me

Gender: Male
Age: 37
Location: Cumbria
Hometown: Keswick
Employment: Computer analyst (self-employed)

Activities and Interests

Fell walking, tropical fish, salsa dancing, family time

Music
Ed Sheeran, Shakira, Luis Fonsi

Books
The Curious Incident of The Dog in The Night-Time, The Power, various biographies

Movies
Guardians of the Galaxy, James Bond, The Greatest Showman

Television
The Apprentice, Mock the Week, Orange Is The New Black

CONNIE

About me

Gender: Female

Age: 64

Location: Gloucestershire

Hometown: Bristol

Employment: Retired

Activities and Interests

Going to the theatre (especially musicals), watching horse racing, travel, my grandchildren, gardening

Music

Michael Bublé, 1960s pop

Books

To Kill A Mockingbird, Stephen King books and crime fiction

Movies

The Best Exotic Marigold Hotel, Les Misérables, La La Land

Television

Downton Abbey, Suits, Poirot

DIGITAL MARKETING

Businesses are keen to understand the digital footprint of their existing and potential customers by collecting information on what they do online, for example, how they use search engines, social media platforms, shopping sites and other websites. This helps them to target different groups of people based on what they search for, buy and look at on online. For example, if you search for concert tickets, you might get adverts for other events and venue information. This is called targeted digital marketing.

QUESTIONS

1. Why do businesses spend vast sums of money on advertising?

2. Why is targeted digital marketing seen as particularly important to advertisers and the companies whose goods they promote?

WAYS TO PAY

The evolution of how we pay for goods and services has taken place over many centuries and new ways are still being developed today. The main ways we pay for the things we buy are:

1. **Cash:** Coins were first used in the 7th century BC and notes first appeared in China a thousand years ago. Many people still use cash today as a quick and convenient way to pay for everyday items – though this is now being challenged by a number of electronic methods.

2. **Cards:** Since they first appeared in the 1950s there has been a rapid growth in the number of plastic cards that can be used to access money. When people want cash nowadays they often use a card at an ATM or cash machine to make a withdrawal. Using plastic is also a popular way of spending, though the two most common types of card can easily (but must not) be confused:

Debit card – When you make a payment or withdraw cash with a debit card, the money is taken straight out of your bank account electronically if you have the money available to spend. You cannot borrow money on a debit card.

Credit card – Available to 18 year olds and older, these allow you to borrow money up to a certain limit. When you buy something with a credit card, the amount you spend is added to the total amount borrowed. (There is much more information on credit cards in the 'Borrowing' chapter.)

One of the benefits of using a credit card is that it gives you greater protection if something goes wrong – for example, the business you bought the goods or services from goes bankrupt, or your order is not delivered. If this happens, then you would be entitled to a refund, but only if the item or service you purchased cost between £100 and £30,000. This protection does not apply to debit cards.

DID YOU KNOW?

The latest significant development with plastic cards is contactless payments, which speed up any transaction. The following symbol identifies that there is a contactless payment option – and is usually found on a card machine or reader.

DISCUSSION

Contactless cards were first introduced in 2007 when the transaction limit was £20 per use. In 2015 this was raised to £30. Research in 2017 showed that more than 50% of retailers thought the limit should be raised to £50 and 20% thought it should be raised to £100.

What are your views on this?

Payments via a bank: If you have a bank account there are a number of payment options open to you, as well as using your debit card. These are:

Electronic transfer – A way of moving money from your account to somebody else's.

Standing order – For paying regular fixed amounts from your bank account automatically. **You are in control** – you instruct your bank to pay the money to a particular person or company. It is your responsibility to change the payment details (e.g. the date or amount) if they need to be changed.

Direct debit – An instruction to your bank to release money from your account to pay bills and other amounts automatically. **The billing company has control** – they request the money from the bank directly, and they can change the amount requested. Some companies, such as gas and electricity, give a discount for paying by this method.

Cheque – Although used far less frequently today, paper cheques are still available as a way to pay for some things.

These methods are widely accepted and are also considered to be secure and safe. However, there are still some risks associated with them – for example, you have to be careful not to make an error when writing out a cheque or setting up a standing order, so always check the details carefully.

4. Digital: The growth of technology has brought with it a number of advanced ways to pay. Among these are:

PayPal – an electronic payments system that allows you to make secure payments to an individual, or to purchase items online.

Mobile phone apps – many UK banks have apps that allow you to transfer money between people or businesses.

Contactless mobile – this allows you to make contactless payments using your phone.

Digital wallets – these are apps that allow you to store all your credit, debit and customer loyalty card details on your phone, so you can choose which payment method you want to use at any time.

Biometric payments – this allows you to make payments using finger scanning technology or facial recognition systems.

Digital ways to pay are convenient as they can usually be used at any time or place. However, the amount you can spend may be limited due to security concerns.

Whichever way you choose to pay for your products and services, always ensure that you use a secure and reliable method of payment and keep all of your cards and details safe. More information about this is covered in the 'Security and fraud' chapter.

DID YOU KNOW?

There have been some interesting items used as money in the past, including shells, cows, stones, blankets and rice.

In 2016, for the very first time, the number of electronic and card payments outstripped payments made by cash. This was driven by a steep rise in the use of contactless payment cards.

Plans to scrap cheques by October 2018 were themselves scrapped when it was shown that over £500m of transactions are still being made using cheques each year!

DISCUSSION

What do you think the next developments in money could be?

Is it possible to have a cashless society?

QUESTIONS

1. What would have been the problem with using goods like shells, cows or stones as a form of payment?

2. Explain the difference between a debit card and a credit card.

3. Explain the difference between a standing order and a direct debit.

4. Which payment methods are the most secure? Explain your answer.

5. In your opinion, does the payment method you use depends on the product or service that you are buying? Explain your answer.

BUDGETING

Budgeting is the process of managing your money. It can be used to manage the balance between your income (the money that comes to you through earnings, gifts, selling things you own, from your parents, etc.) and your outgoings (your expenditure, savings, etc.).

A budget is the best way to keep your finances in check and to make sure you achieve what you want to achieve with your money. It ensures that:

• You have enough money to cover the necessities

• You are spending on what really matters to you

• You are putting money aside for the future

• You have considered other things you might want to use your money for, such as giving to charity.

 THE BUDGETING PROCESS

Budgeting does not have to be complicated. In its simplest form, it is a list of what you need/want to spend compared against a list of what income you have.

Look at Robyn's weekly budget below. As you can see, she expects to earn £94.63 per week from her part time job and allowance and expects to spend £84.19 per week on various outgoings.

Robyn's weekly budget

INCOME	EXPENDITURE
£54.63 part time job	£8 cinema
£40 allowance	£22.46 lunch out
	£7.49 film download
	£38.99 jeans
	£7.25 bus trips
TOTAL £94.63	TOTAL £84.19

 DID YOU KNOW?

The Chancellor of the Exchequer presents the national budget to government once a year, which details how the UK's income will be spent.

DISCUSSION

In the example, Robyn's spending (expenditure) is lower than her income. What could she do with the difference?

What if it was the other way around and her expenditure was greater than her income?

As people get older, especially when they start living on their own, their level of 'committed' spending (spending they need to make) can increase. Depending on their level of income they may then need to cut back on their 'discretionary' spending (spending they don't need to make but might want to).

Examples of committed and discretionary spending

COMMITTED SPENDING	DISCRETIONARY SPENDING
Mortgage or rent	Digital TV/internet packages
Utilities (e.g. gas, electricity, water)	Gym membership
Food	Subscriptions
Car running costs (e.g. petrol)	Entertainment (e.g. cinema, theatre, going out to eat)
Insurance (e.g. car, home, life)	Days out
TV licence	Holidays

 ## DISCUSSION

What heading would you put your phone under? Is this committed or discretionary spending?

A budget is not something that always stays the same. As your financial situation changes, so can your budget. With a little more income, you might make different spending choices, but equally, you might need to cut back on spending if it does not match your income.

CASE STUDY

Awurabena recently got her first job after university on a graduate training scheme with an engineering company. To take up this opportunity, she had to move away from home. At university she shared a house with five other people, but now she is working Awurabena decided she would rather rent a flat of her own.

Awurabena is paid £1,540 per month. This more than covers the £550 rent on her flat, but she was a little more surprised at some of the other costs associated with living on her own. Her gas and electricity cost her around £65 a month, the water bill works out to be £27.50 a month, and she spends an average of £55 on her weekly food shop. In addition to these costs, she subscribes to a music and movie app which, combined, cost her £19 a month, and she also pays £23.87 a month to insure her belongings in the flat.

As well as the costs associated with her flat,

Awurabena tries to go out with her work colleagues at least twice a week, costing on average £60 a week. As a reward for getting her new job she upgraded her mobile and now pays £34 a month for a new model.

One thing Awurabena hadn't anticipated were the costs associated with her new job – travelling to work (£78 a week), buying appropriate clothes (around £90 a month) and buying a coffee every morning (£12.50 a week).

Awurabena is looking at buying a second hand car to travel to work instead of using the train. To be able to do this she has worked out she needs to save £150 a month for a year.

- Use the information about Awurabena to create a monthly budget for her. (TOP TIP – you could use Robyn's budget as a template to help you.)

- Consider whether Awurabena can begin to save for her car and, if not, suggest ways she could amend her budget so that she could.

Managing a budget is a good way of making sure you don't spend more than your income. A budget will also help to show you if there is room to save any money. By cutting down on some of your spending you may well be able to save some money on a regular basis.

Top tips for managing a budget:

- Look more than just one month into the future. The further ahead you are able to plan a budget for, the better.

- Remember to update your budget to include costs around key events such as birthdays, Christmas, Eid, Rosh Hashanah, etc.

- Use your bank statements to monitor your actual spending. If you can do this in 'real time' using mobile or online banking, rather than at the end of the month, even better.

 DISCUSSION

Think of two reasons why a family might have to spend more money in one month than they were planning to.

What changes might they make to their expenditure if these situations happened?

- Stick to the budget. It's fairly easy to write a budget, but the harder part is making sure you stick to it. There will always be things that change, but adjust your budget accordingly, and keep to it.

QUESTIONS

1. Give two examples of income and two examples of expenditure.

2. What are two options you have if you find you have gone "over budget"?

3. Why does budgeting need to be more than a one-off activity?

KEEPING TRACK OF YOUR BUDGET

Setting a budget is one thing but sticking to it is just as important. There are various ways in which you can do this, but we will look at three easy ways to keep track of everyday income and expenditure:

1. Multiple money pots

One of the reasons that sticking to a budget can be so difficult is that the majority of your income tends to all be held in just one place – that could be a moneybox at home, or a current account with a bank. All of your spending then has to come from just one place too, and that can make it difficult to see exactly how much you are spending on certain types of things, e.g. going out, clothes, food etc.

The money pot method of budgeting suggests that you separate your income into different spending pots – these could be separate money boxes at home, or even separate bank accounts. This means you can allocate you budget to the different money pots at the beginning of the month, and you'll always know how much you have left for different types of spending.

The trick to using this method is to get the amount of money right for each 'pot' and then that tells you how much you have left to spend on those things.

2. Manage a cash book

A cash book is simply a way of recording money that is received or spent. By doing this every time there is a transaction the balance of money available is kept up to date. Although it's called a cash book you can use this method to record any form of transaction, such as direct debits and electronic payments.

There are some simple steps to maintaining a cashbook:

DISCUSSION

If your income for a month was £130, how would you split this across the following spending pots

- Going out
- Clothes
- Food
- Travel

Firstly, you need to set up your template, which always includes the following headings (this can be on paper or electronically using Excel):

DATE	DESCRIPTION	INCOME	EXPENDITURE	BALANCE

Next, you'll need to work out your 'opening balance'. This is how much money you have at the point you are starting the cash book (if it's nothing, that's fine – your opening balance will be £0.00).

Finally, you need to record any income or expenditure that occurs, providing the date and a description of the transaction into the cash book. Every time you do this you will need to write in the new balance. Any income received will increase the balance, and any new expenditure will reduce the balance.

Example:

DATE	TYPE	DESCRIPTION	INCOME	EXPENDITURE	BALANCE	CHECK TO BANK STATEMENT
1.10.18		Opening balance			23.45	
2.10.18	CR	Allowance	40.00		63.45	✓
5.10.18	CQ	New jeans		34.99	28.46	✓
8.10.18	CR	Part time pay	76.98		105.44	✓
9.10.18	DC	Train travel		16.53	88.91	✓
14.10.18	CM	Cash		20.00	63.96	✓
18.10.18	DC	Lunch out		15.76	48.20	✓
25.10.18	DC	Cinema trip		12.99	35.21	
29.10.18	DC	New bag		23.45	11.76	

DC – Debit card CM – Cash machine CR – Cash receipt CQ – Cheque

From the example above, you can see that maintaining the cash book enables you to see exactly how much money you have left.

If you use a back account you can also use your bank statement to check that the cash book is correct. This is simply a case of ticking off every transaction on your bank statement against the equivalent record in your cash book. If there are items on the bank statement not in your cash book, these can then be added to the cash book. Reconciling the balance in the bank statement to the balance on the cash book can then be done as follows:

Imagine you had forgotten to add the last two entries on your cash book. The balance per your cash book would be £48.20, but your bank statement would show £11.76.

Looking at your bank statement you would see two items not yet included in your cash book:

Cinema trip £12.99   New bag £23.45

By adding them in, the balance of your cash book would be £11.76 – the same as your bank statement.

Whilst you can choose the period your cash book covers, they are usually displayed either weekly or monthly. As with the multiple money pots method you can track your spending across different categories to make sure you are sticking within your budget.

ACTIVITY

Use the following information to compete a cash book for Jayne:

July is a big month for Jayne – it's her birthday, and she has a music festival to go to. She begins the month with £26.50 and receives £80 for her birthday on the 2nd July. On the 5th July she spends £35.67 on clothing, ready for the festival. The following day she buys her train tickets in advance for £25.65. On the 14th July, her nan gives her £20 for helping her with the gardening. The first day of the festival is 20th July and Jayne spends £12.32 on food and drink. The following day she spends £13.45 on food and drink and £15.56 on the third day.

3. Using budgeting apps

There are now many apps which use the principal of a cash book and combine this with innovations in technology to provide some really powerful tools to help you keep track of your budgeting.

These apps can synchronise with your bank account (or more than one if that's the case) and will automatically display the income and expenditure transactions and overall balance you have available (just like a cash book).

Where these apps can be extremely useful though is in automatically categorising the types of transactions you make (such as on clothing, food or going out) and displaying the total amount spent in a given period. They can also show the spending on each category as a percentage of your total income, making it really clear how you are choosing to spend your money, and possibly where you might want to make changes.

VALUE FOR MONEY

The word "budget" can also mean less expensive – as in the term "budget airline". One way of staying within your means is to look at using cheaper alternatives to what you might usually buy. Something which is cheaper may have just as much value as a more expensive option, and the feeling that you are getting good value for money can be very positive. Price is not necessarily a guarantee of quality or value. This is why it is so important to do your own research, read articles and reviews, and compare prices, deals and offers.

 ## ACTIVITY

Use the information in the table below to calculate the savings that can be made just by switching the type of brand you buy.

1. Work out the cost per week of each product for each of the three brand types.

2. Work out the saving difference **per week** between:

    a) Luxury and supermarket own brand

    b) Between luxury and value range

3. Work out the cost **per year** (52 weeks in a year) of each product for each of the three brand types.

4. Work out the saving difference **per year** between:

    a) Luxury and supermarket own brand

    b) Luxury and value range

PRODUCT	NUMBER BOUGHT PER WEEK	LUXURY BRAND	SUPERMARKET OWN BRAND	VALUE RANGE
Can of baked beans	4	£1.04	£0.65	£0.23
Cereal	1	£3.65	£2.21	£1.68
Crisps	6	£1.20	£0.99	£0.45
Batteries	2	£3.95	£2.89	£0.99

SHOPPING AROUND

You can often buy the same product from different places at different prices, and in some cases very different prices. To ensure you are getting a good deal, it can pay to shop around. While you could walk up and down the High Street looking in each shop, the internet provides some simple solutions to comparing prices:

1. **Using price comparison websites.** These have been developed specifically to compare the prices of goods from a range of suppliers and retailers. You enter what you are looking for and they will provide you with a range of options. They're a very useful tool, but it is worth remembering that these sites do not usually represent all the suppliers, and the supplier with the best price might be online only, or not one you recognise. Also, be aware that different comparison websites will often show different prices for the same product, so make sure to compare comparison websites too!

2. **Explore online before hitting the High Street.** Comparing a few stores online before heading to the shops will save you from achy feet and it is a good way of comparing a range of shops to see which has the best price. You might also spot exclusive online deals and offers too.

3. **Information and review sites can be really useful.** They can help you understand the product you are interested in to make sure it meets your needs. Review sites can be very helpful in seeing the opinions of others on the product you are interested in. This could help you identify any issues with quality or value for money. Remember, just because a product is more expensive, it doesn't mean it is better quality.

4. **Renegotiate renewals and other contracts.** Never renew a mobile phone contract at the same price straightaway, as it is always worth checking on a comparison site to see if you can get a deal cheaper elsewhere. You can always contact your current provider to see if they can beat the quotes too. This is the same for TV, broadband, utilities and insurance – always make sure you are getting the best contract terms for your needs.

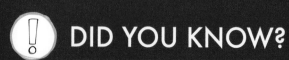

DID YOU KNOW?

Comparison websites first appeared in the mid-1990s. They are basically search engines that shoppers can use to filter and compare products based on price and other factors. They don't usually directly sell products themselves; instead they earn money from marketing agreements with the companies they are working with.

COMPARING PRICES IN THE SUPERMARKET

If you are going to the supermarket, look for the unit price of goods to work out the best deals. The unit price is the cost per litre, kilogram, etc., of something you are looking to buy. While one product might look more expensive than another, if you are getting more of it, it might be better value.

DID YOU KNOW?

There are price comparison apps you can use that allow you to scan a product's barcode to find out if you can buy it cheaper elsewhere.

ACTIVITY

What are the best deals here?

The chicken and the egg or cheep versus cheap!

- A 200g chicken for £4.50
- A 500g chicken for £6.00
- A 1kg chicken for £10.00

- A box of 12 eggs for £3.80
- A box of 9 eggs for £2.70
- A box of 6 eggs for £2.20

When considering unit price, it is important to think about whether you actually need it all or not. There is no point in buying a box of 9 eggs if you are only going to use 3 and the rest go bad; this would mean the unit price per useful egg would be much higher.

DISCUSSION

Consider some situations in which you might be tempted to pay a bit more for something rather than opt for the cheapest deal.

QUESTIONS

1. What are two different uses of the word "budget"?

2. Why should you try and use more than one comparison site when researching prices?

3. How does knowing the unit price of something help a consumer?

KNOW YOUR RIGHTS

We all like to get a good deal, and making sure you get value for money is important, but what happens if something goes wrong? What if the item you searched hard for and ordered online does not arrive, or you find the bargain top you picked up has a hole in it when you get home?

Well, in nearly all cases you are protected by your consumer rights. These cover a whole range of situations where there could be problems with the goods and services you have bought. Very simply, when you buy any good or services they should:

Last a reasonable length of time

be **O**f satisfactory quality

be **A**s described

be **F**it for purpose

Use your **LOAF** when buying goods and services!

If the good or service you buy does not fit with one or more of the LOAF definitions then you are protected by the Consumer Rights Act 2015. If you return the item within 30 days, you are entitled to a full refund. You can still return the item after this, but the supplier can then offer a repair or replacement instead (and then a full or partial refund if this does not work).

BEWARE! If you buy a product from a shop (not online) and make a mistake – for example, you don't like it when you get home, or it doesn't fit with your colour scheme – this is your fault and there is no obligation for the retailer to provide a refund or exchange the product.

DID YOU KNOW?

Many retailers will give longer returns periods, and more enhanced terms than the law states. What is in the Consumer Rights Act 2015 is the bare minimum.

BUYING ON THE INTERNET

When you buy something on the internet you are still covered by the Consumer Rights Act. LOAF still applies, but there is additional protection through the Consumer Contracts Regulation 2013.

You have a right to cancel (even if you just change your mind):

- For goods, this is up to 14 days after you receive the goods (you then have 14 more days to return them)

- For services, it is 14 days after the day you placed the order

QUESTIONS

1. What are the four things it is your right to expect from a good or a service?

2. What is the difference in law between returning a faulty good within 30 days and after 30 days?

WHAT HAVE YOU LEARNT?

Using the knowledge you have gained from this chapter, complete the activity and case study below:

ACTIVITY

Create a social media "top tips" list, noting the key points you think are important about making good money decisions. You could include information about:

- Best ways to pay
- Benefits of budgeting
- How to get good value for money.

CASE STUDY

Samira is 18 and wants to buy a brand-new laptop for college. She has seen the one she wants and it has been reviewed online by one of her favourite vloggers. It costs £550.

However, her parents have suggested that she look at alternative models as they might offer everything she wants but at a cheaper price.

1. Identify two influences on Samira's spending.

2. Recommend how Samira could get the best value for money by shopping around.

3. If the laptop breaks down, what are Samira's consumer rights?

4. Considering all of the different ways to pay, decide how Samira should pay for her laptop. Explain your answer.

FURTHER
YOUR KNOWLEDGE

OVERSPEND ON BUDGET

Consider this monthly budget for a 20-year-old single male. Rav is currently spending more than he earns in income. Work out how much he needs to reduce his spending by to 'break even' and have his income match his expenditure.

Rav is not able to increase his income, so must reduce his spending. Re-write his budget showing where you would reduce his expenditure. For each reduction in expenditure you should also give an explanation for why you made the change.

INCOME	EXPENDITURE	
Wages as a fitness instructor **£1,200**	Rent	**£520**
	Council tax	**£117**
Fees as a personal trainer **£590**	Gas/electric	**£97**
	Water	**£32**
	Telephone/internet	**£26**
	TV license	**£13**
	Insurance	**£33**
	Credit card balance	**£217**
	Groceries and cleaning materials	**£95**
	Travel	**£62**
	Clothes	**£150**
	Laundry and dry cleaning	**£66**
	Sport activities (inc. football season ticket)	**£104**
	Toiletries and personal grooming	**£68**
	Mobile phone (inc. apps)	**£71**
	Nights out	**£275**
	Other treats (e.g. coffees, computer games)	**£170**
	Presents for other people	**£25**
	Sundries	**£35**
Total income:	Total expenditure:	

VALUE FOR MONEY

In 2016, a survey conducted by the Money Advice Service tested 2,000 customers on their shopping "savviness". Surprisingly, only 2% managed to get all the questions right. Now see how you do.

1. Of the following options for milk, which represents the best deal?

a) Six pints of milk for £1.80

b) Four pints of milk for £1.40

c) Two 6-pint cartons of milk on offer for £3.50

d) Two 4-pint cartons of milk on offer for £2

2. Of the following options for buying 500g of lemons, which represents the best deal?

a) One 500g pack of lemons costing £1.20

b) 500g of loose lemons at £2.50 per kilo

c) Buy two get the third free deal on 200g packs of lemons costing 70p each

d) Buy one get one half price deal on 250g packs of lemons costing 70p each

3. Of the following options for buying tomato ketchup, which represents the best deal?

a) One 460g bottle on offer at £1.50

b) One 910g bottle costing £2.49

c) Buy one get one half price deal on 700g bottles costing £2.29 each

d) One 1.35kg bottle costing £3.50

4. Of the following options for buying eggs, which represents the best deal?

a) Six medium eggs for £1.10

b) 10 medium eggs on offer for £1.50

c) 15 medium eggs for £2.10

d) Two packs of six medium eggs on offer for £2

e) Buy one get one free offer on packs of 10 medium eggs priced at £2.20

Money Advice Service, 2016

CONSUMER RIGHTS

Read the following statements about your rights as a consumer and decide whether they are true (T) or false (F). If the statement is true add further explanatory notes; if it is false, rewrite the statement accurately. Use **www.moneysavingexpert.com/shopping/consumer-rights-refunds-exchange** for your research.

	T	F	
You have bought a kettle in a store sale and it is not heating the water. The store tells you that you should complain to the manufacturer.			
When buying a T-shirt in a store you have accidentally picked up the wrong size. Your neighbour, who works in the retail sector, tells you that the shop does not have to exchange it.			
You have used your debit card to purchase a pair of trainers but when you get home you find the sole of one of them is coming unstuck. However, you have lost the receipt so that means you won't be able to return them.			
You have ordered a necklace online to wear at your 18th birthday party. The agreed delivery date is on the big day, but it actually arrives the day after. You are entitled to a full refund.			
A book you have been after has turned up in an online auction advertised by a private seller. You buy the book but when it arrives you discover it is one you have already read before. However, you are sure you have the same right of return as buying it in a bookstore, so it can be sent back to the seller.			
The holiday company you are dealing with goes bust and you lose all the hard-earned money you have paid out to it. A friend tells you that you should have used a credit card for this purchase.			

BORROWING
HOW DO I MAKE BORROWING CHOICES?

In this chapter you will explore options about borrowing money.

You will see how borrowing has increasingly become a part of the modern world, and that it requires very careful management.

You will look at the various ways there are to borrow money and what the advantages and disadvantages are of each method. You will also investigate how repayments and interest work.

Failure to repay and getting into debt can have serious consequences, so you will be looking at how to avoid these situations and what to do if debt does build up.

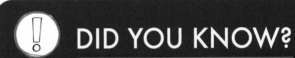

DID YOU KNOW?

Debt is essentially borrowing against your future income. You are choosing to have money now that you will then repay out of your future income, but you will also pay an extra cost because you're borrowing it.

BORROWING AND DEBT

Borrowing is receiving money from someone else with the agreement that you will pay it back at a later date. You might borrow informally from friends and family or take out a formal loan with a written agreement from a bank or building society. If interest charges are added to money that is borrowed, you will pay more back than the initial amount borrowed.

Loans and borrowing are now a part of modern life; they have become almost unavoidable in one form or another. You have to be at least 18 years old to borrow from banks but there are a lot of different forms of borrowing to choose from, for example:

- Organising a bank overdraft to help your monthly budgeting

- Using hire purchase to buy a car

- Taking out a personal loan to fund a one-off payment

- Borrowing via a student loan to help fund yourself through higher education

- Arranging a mortgage to buy a property

- Using a credit card to pay when shopping online.

You will find out a lot more about these different forms of borrowing later in the chapter.

DID YOU KNOW?

By late 2017:

- **People in the UK owed £1.566 trillion – that's £1,566,000,000**

- **£1.36 trillion of that is outstanding mortgage debt**

- **That is an average debt of £30,253 per adult (including mortgage debt) – around 114% of average earnings**

- **This debt is predicted to reach £2.296 trillion by 2022**

- **The number of debt problems dealt with by Citizens Advice every day was 4,563.**

Source: The Money Charity, The Money Statistics January 2018

SO, DEBT MUST BE BAD, RIGHT?

It's a common misconception that all debt is "bad". There are a number of circumstances where borrowing can be used to help us buy things which will have a positive impact on our lives and even improve our financial position over time. For example, borrowing money to buy a home. By taking out a mortgage you are buying your home and it becomes yours to own when the mortgage is paid off – unlike renting, where you may be making a similar payment but never own the property. Over time you would also hope that the value of the home increases, so that when you come to sell the property it would be worth more than you had initially borrowed. However you would need to bear in mind that property values may fall as well as rise.

The reasons for taking on debt can be described as "good" or "bad", depending on what you borrow the money for:

- Good debt will provide an ongoing benefit to the borrower or will result in some kind of financial return

- Bad debt does not provide ongoing benefit or a financial return to the borrower.

 GOOD OR BAD – MAKE SURE IT'S MANAGEABLE

Whether the reason for the debt is deemed to be good or bad, the borrower must make sure that they can afford to pay it back. This usually means the borrower has budgeted for the repayment of the debt and has sufficient regular income to cover the cost. In this case, the debt would be called **manageable debt**.

If a debt is taken on with no means to repay it, then this is called **unmanageable debt**.

The difference between manageable and unmanageable debt is not always straightforward as people's situations can change. Imagine someone who took out a debt they could manage and afford then loses their job. Very quickly, the once manageable debt can become unmanageable.

You will explore more about manageable and unmanageable debt later in the chapter.

 ## ACTIVITY

Look at the list below and identify those that would be classed as "good" debt and those classed as "bad" debt.

Borrowing to:

- Go on an exotic holiday

- Buy a car to travel to work each day

- Buy a house to live in

- Get a wardrobe full of new clothes

- Fund higher education

- Get festival tickets

 ## QUESTIONS:

1. Name three different forms of borrowing.

2. What is meant by good and bad debt?

3. How is good and bad debt different to manageable and unmanageable debt'?

REPAYMENT, INTEREST AND APR

 ## REPAYING THE DEBT

When money is borrowed it has to be repaid. In fact, there are three things which have to be repaid:

- The original sum borrowed (known as the Principal)
- Interest which is added to the principal
- Any charges or fees connected to the loan of the principal.

When you borrow money from a bank they will add interest onto the amount you have borrowed. This is the bank's reward for lending you the money.

The formula for calculating simple interest is:

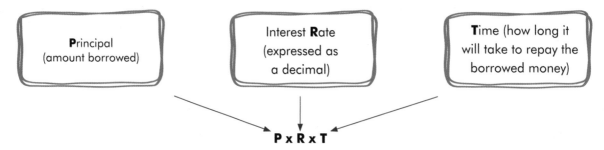

For example, if £1,000 is borrowed at an interest rate of 20% over 1 year, then the interest to be repaid would be:

£1,000 x 0.2 x 1 = £200

The total repayment to the lender would be:

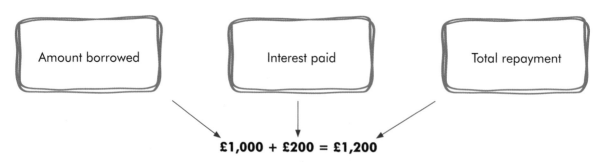

 ## DID YOU KNOW?

The official UK interest rate (often called the base rate) is reviewed and set eight times a year by the Bank of England. Many financial companies link individual interest rates for some of their products (e.g. mortgages) to rises and falls in the base rate.

ACTIVITY

Using the repayment formula on the left, calculate the total amount that would need to be repaid if borrowing £3,000 for 1 year at the following rates:

1. 8%   **2.** 25.5%   **3.** 36.8%   **4.** 1,499% (payday lenders really do charge this much!)

COMPOUND INTEREST

Calculating the interest on borrowing over longer periods is slightly more complicated as banks will use a calculation known as compound interest. This recognises that at the end of year 1, the total amount you owe will be the principal plus the interest for that year. This means that the interest for year 2 is calculated on the total (principal plus interest) owed at the end of year 1.

So, if the £1,000 is borrowed for 3 years and the 20% rate is compounded it will work out as follows:

Year 1: 1,000 x 0.20 x 1 = £200   Total owed at the end of Year 1 = £1,200

Year 2: 1,200 x 0.20 x 1 = £240   Total owed at the end of Year 2 = £1,440

Year 3: 1,440.00 x 0.20 x 1 = £288   Total at the end of Year 3 = £1,728

So, if £1,000 were borrowed at an interest rate of 20% you would need to pay **£1,728** to repay it after 3 years.

Imagine if the borrowing term was over many more years, the method above would take quite a long time to calculate and just like in the 'Saving' chapter, we can also use the multiplier method. For example, if £15,000 was borrowed over 7 years at an interest rate of 9%, the total amount repayable would be:

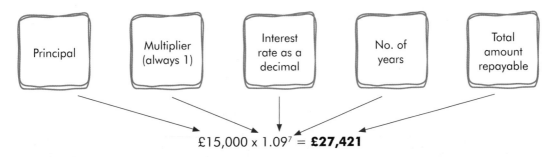

$$£15,000 \times 1.09^7 = £27,421$$

Be aware that the formulas we have looked at assume that there are no repayments being made until the very end of the borrowing period. In reality, this is not the case, and you usually make regular repayments against the borrowing. For example, you might repay £200 a month against your loan.

What effect do you think this will have on the interest you pay?

The formula for compound interest can be found in the 'Saving' chapter.

ACTIVITY

Using the compound interest formula, calculate the total amount that would need to be repaid if borrowing £3,000 at an interest rate of 20% over the following periods:

1. 2 years   **2.** 4 years

3. 7 years   **4.** 15 years

Now try...

5. 3 months   **6.** 6 months

INTEREST RATES CAN CHANGE

When borrowing or saving it is possible the rate of interest might change. The impact this has on you depends on the type of borrowing you have, for example:

- Fixed-rate borrowing will guarantee the same interest rate for either a specified time period of the loan or the full loan period.

- Variable-rate borrowing means that interest payments may change if the lender changes their rate.

ACTIVITY

1. Using the definitions of fixed-rate and variable-rate borrowing, explain one advantage and disadvantage of each.

2. Consider what the impact would be for people with variable-rate borrowing of:

- A rise in interest rates

- A fall in interest rates

3. What if they had fixed rate borrowing?

CASE STUDY

Caz and Jenny have seen a flat they want to buy which is on the market for £150,000. They have managed to save £20,000 for a deposit so need to take out a mortgage of £130,000, which they intend to repay over 25 years (300 months). They have shopped around and need to make a final decision between the two deals below:

Option 1 – 2 year fixed rate mortgage

For the first 2 years (24 months) they will repay at a fixed rate of 1.99%, which is £550.38 per month. After the 2 year period is up, they will go onto a variable rate for the remaining 23 years (276 months), which is currently 4.49% and £709.77 per month.

Option 2 – variable rate mortgage

Throughout the whole 25 years (300 months) they would repay the mortgage at a variable rate. This is currently 4.14% and £696.28 per month although, being a variable rate, it can go up or down, making the monthly payments increase or decrease accordingly.

1. By simply looking at the two options, which one would you choose and why?

2. If the interest rates stayed the same throughout the lifetime of the mortgages, what would be the total amounts repayable for each option?

3. Based on the answers to question two, which option should Caz and Jenny choose?

4. Realistically, why might this not be the best option in the long run?

5. Knowing this, does this affect your choice of mortgage for Caz and Jenny? Explain your answer.

APR

APR stands for Annual Percentage Rate and is shown as a percentage. Remember, at the start of this chapter, we said that the amount you repay is made up of the amount you borrowed (or principal), the interest rate, and any charges or fees the lender makes.

The APR takes into account any fees and charges attached to the loan over 1 year, as well as the interest rate being charged, and shows it all as one percentage figure. The idea is that it makes it much easier to compare the costs of borrowing from different providers or using different forms of borrowing.

You should always see the APR figure stated on any advertising for borrowing products. However, what you will see in such adverts is a "typical" or "representative" APR – the actual rate you receive will take into account your personal circumstances. For example, if the bank considers lending to you to be slightly risky they might increase the interest rate, which also increases the APR.

The interest rate you receive when you save money in an account (taking into account any associated fees and charges) is known as the Annual Equivalent Rate (AER). Make sure you don't get these confused!

 DID YOU KNOW!

The interest banks pay on your savings is often lower than the rate they charge for borrowing. The difference between the rates is the profit the bank makes – they are a business after all!

 DID YOU KNOW!

Islamic Sharia law expressly forbids the charging of interest on loans, which is known as usury. It is believed that wealth should be generated only through trade and investment. There are specialist financial products available which are Sharia compliant.

 DISCUSSION

Only 51% of successful applicants need to be given the representative APR for a lender to be allowed to advertise it. Many customers will most likely be offered a higher rate.

Why do you think lenders advertise borrowing products with representative APR if not all customers will be given it?

 QUESTIONS:

1. What are the three elements of repayment?

2. Explain the difference between APR and AER.

3. How might changes in the UK base rate of interest affect borrowers?

MAKING INFORMED CHOICES

Most people will have to borrow money at some point in their lives so understanding the choices you have, and the consequences of your actions, is essential.

CASE STUDY

Kofi wants to buy a second hand car to make his journey to work easier. He has found one he likes, costing £3,250. He has just about that amount in savings, but that is all of his savings, and he has been setting this aside for a deposit on a new flat. Having written a budget, Kofi has worked out he is able to put around £190 into savings each month. He has decided he has three options:

- Use existing savings
- Save up for it
- Borrow the money.

Consider each of the options for Kofi. What are the advantages and disadvantages of each?

Is there anything further you would like to know before making the final decision?

HOW BANKS MAKE DECISIONS

While we all have to make decisions about whether to borrow or not, which product meets our needs the best, and who offers the product at the best APR, the organisations who are lending the money also have to make their own decisions. The discussion below will help you consider the decisions they have to make.

DISCUSSION

Imagine you are the bank. A customer comes in looking to borrow £5,000 over 2 years.

What do you want to know before making your decision on whether to lend the customer the money or not?

CREDIT HISTORY

One of the tools a bank uses to make their lending decisions is to look at your credit history – how much money you have borrowed in the past, and how you have managed it. This is in the form of something called a credit report, which gives details of each borrowing product you have taken out, the repayments you have made, whether any repayment dates have been missed, and the level of outstanding credit (debt) you have.

When you apply to borrow money, the lender will usually ask your permission to access your credit report. These are provided to the lender by a credit reference agency. It is the credit reference agency that collects all of the information on you and forms it into a report. They then provide these to the lender when a new borrowing application is made. The lender will use this information to decide whether they are able to lend to you, and if so, at what APR.

Your credit history is really important to ensuring the best borrowing rates are offered to you. There are some key tips to making sure your credit history is maintained positively:

- Stick to repayment schedules. Missed payments will show up on your credit report and may make a lender question your ability to repay on time.

- Don't make too many borrowing applications at the same time. As well as recording your past and present borrowing, your credit history also records the number of applications you have made. If a lender sees too many applications, they may consider you too risky to lend to.

- Build a credit history. This one may sound a little strange! Consider if you were the bank and someone asks to borrow quite a large amount of money. You look at their credit history and find it's blank – nothing there. You would not know how the person will manage the borrowing as there is nothing to base it on.

Some people actively build a credit history by taking out borrowing products such as credit cards, using them occasionally and making sure they are repaid on time and before any interest is charged.

As well as reviewing your credit history, lenders may also make their decision based on "affordability". By looking at your income and expenditure they will work out how much to lend to you based on what they think you can pay back. If you have a good credit history, but the lender doesn't think you can afford the repayments, you might not be able to borrow as much as you wanted.

Definitions

Credit history – A record of loans you have taken out or credit card payments made or missed. This information is stored by credit reference agencies, who supply details of your credit history to financial institutions when you take out further loans.

Credit reference agency – An agency that holds information on adults, including public records (e.g. electoral register entries) and credit history information. They make this information available to lenders when you apply for credit, who then use the information to decide whether or not to offer you credit.

Credit report – A detailed report of an individual's credit history, current credit arrangements, address history and details of anyone you are financially linked with. When you apply for credit, the process usually involves you giving your permission to the credit provider (e.g. banks, credit card providers, mobile phone companies) to check your credit report.

Credit score – Lenders will use your credit history to calculate a credit score which reflects the level of risk in lending to you and the likelihood of you paying credit back. Each lender scores you differently, and secretly, so if one lender has rejected you, it doesn't automatically mean others will. After a rejection it's always important to check your credit report for any errors before applying for credit again.

QUESTIONS:

1. What are the decisions that lending organisations have to make before giving credit to a customer?

2. What tools do lenders use to help them make these decisions?

3. Name two ways that you can help build a positive credit history.

BORROWING PRODUCTS

 DID YOU KNOW?

Loans can be secured or unsecured. A secured loan requires something that gives the lender security in case you cannot pay the loan back. This is usually your home but could also be a guarantor. A guarantor is a person who agrees to be responsible for the loan if you cannot make the repayments. If you fail to repay the loan, the bank can get their money back by selling the security or requesting the guarantor pays.

An unsecured loan does not involve security, but as the lender is taking a greater risk the APR tends to be higher.

Borrowing comes in many different forms. Here are some of the main ones:

BORROWING METHOD	DEFINITION	ADVANTAGES	DISADVANTAGES
Personal loan	When money is borrowed for a non-specified purpose and generally paid back in monthly instalments.	• You repay the same amount every month, which helps with budgeting.	• May take a long time to pay off, depending on the amount borrowed and the APR.
Credit card	A plastic card issued by a financial organisation with a certain limit agreed or prearranged to allow you to spend (borrow) money up to that amount. If you do not pay off the full amount each month you will start paying interest on it.	• Better consumer protection if something goes wrong • May get a 0% or low interest card for an introductory period.	• Can encourage overspending if the money available is seen as extra cash • Interest rates can increase.
Store card	Store cards are like credit cards but are available from shops rather than banks. They can only be used to buy things at particular shops. Anything you spend on your store card is borrowed money and, as with credit cards, if you do not pay off the full amount each month you will start paying interest on it.	• A shopper may be given the incentive of a discount on an opening purchase or similar offer.	• Usually very expensive if the balance is not repaid in full.

Overdraft	An overdraft allows you to borrow money through your current account. They can be requested from the bank or are sometimes automatically offered with current accounts. Arranged overdrafts are set in advance and you can spend money up to the agreed overdraft amount.	• Provides a short-term solution • If arranged, can be paid off without penalties • Only pay interest if the overdraft is used.	• There may be fees to pay for authorised overdrafts • If you go overdrawn without asking the bank in advance or have an arranged overdraft and spend more than the amount agreed, this is an unarranged overdraft • In this case the bank will almost certainly penalise you with additional fees and charge you a higher interest rate on the money that you owe them.
Hire purchase	Tends to be for larger purchases, e.g. a car. Repayments take place regularly over a number of years, but you do not legally own whatever you have purchased until the final repayment has been made.	• Allows you to purchase new things that you could not otherwise afford • Spreads the cost of an expensive item over a period of time.	• Failure to repay means the goods can be legally taken away from you • Until paid for, you cannot sell the goods on or alter them in any way.
Student loan (this will be covered in greater detail in the 'Moving on from school – world of work' chapter)	Specifically designed to fund you through higher education and is then repaid regularly after you start work.	• You only start to make repayments once you start earning over a certain amount • Low interest rates.	• Repayments will be considered as part of affordability checks for a mortgage • The government is able to change the repayment threshold and interest rate.
Mortgage	Used to purchase property or land and usually takes many years to repay.	• Allows you to spread the cost of property over a long period of time.	• Changes in interest rates can affect repayments • Failure to make repayments may affect your credit rating and continuing to do so may ultimately mean you lose your home.

Alternative credit: This covers catalogue shopping, doorstep money lenders, rent to own shops, pawnbrokers and payday loan companies, where the interest rates tend to be very high, so borrowing is very costly. These methods may be used by people with a poor credit history, meaning they are unable to borrow money at more competitive rates.

Remember, the higher the APR the more it will cost you to borrow, and the longer you borrow for at the same APR the more it will cost you.

CREDIT UNIONS

Credit unions are financial co-operatives, owned and controlled by their members, which offer a local alternative to banks and building societies. They are often run by members of a local community and the members who use their services can help make decisions about how the credit union is managed.

They are not-for-profit organisations that offer similar financial products and services to banks or building societies, for example, personal loans and savings accounts. They have a social responsibility to support their local community and they try to ensure that costs are kept low so that borrowing rates are often lower than alternative credit providers. They can also allow for higher interest rates on savings. This can often mean that people who are unable to access high street banks and their products have financial support in their community, offering a good alternative to payday loans and doorstep lending.

ACTIVITY

Carry out research on credit unions and payday lenders and write some bullet points about what you have discovered. Consider including:

- What products they offer
- What their interest rates are
- How they differ from banks
- The pros and cons of each

QUESTIONS:

1. What is the difference between a credit card and a store card?

2. Why do people sometimes turn to alternative credit providers?

3. Explain the difference between an arranged overdraft and an unarranged overdraft.

4. What are the differences of using a credit union rather than a bank?

PERSONAL LOANS

A personal loan is an agreement between an individual (the borrower) and the financial organisation which is supplying the money (the lender).

Personal loans are usually taken out for a term of between 1 and 10 years and are usually unsecured (read the previous 'Did you know' to find out the difference between secured and unsecured borrowing).

You can apply for a personal loan through a bank, building society, credit union or an online financial company. Each will advertise their interest as a "typical" or "representative" APR, but remember, this may not be the rate you actually receive as it will be based on your individual circumstances.

On agreement, you will be provided with a repayment schedule. This shows all the repayments you will need to make over the term of the loan – these are usually monthly but can vary according to the Terms and Conditions of the loan. Once you are happy with the agreement, you will be asked to sign a contract and the money will be transferred to your bank account.

DID YOU KNOW?

Terms and Conditions (T&Cs) are often called "the small print" and are the set of rules surrounding your loan. These should be carefully checked to make sure you are getting what you expected. In signing the contract, you are also agreeing to the T&Cs – although there is a 14-day "cooling off" period before they become legally binding.

At each repayment instalment you will be paying back a set sum made up of some of the principal (original loan amount) and some of the interest. This continues until the entire borrowed sum and the interest have been repaid.

If you have made some payments and then want to pay off the remaining amount (balance) of the loan early, a company will sometimes charge an early repayment charge (ERC), which may take the total to more than you would have paid over the agreed amount of time. They do this because they will otherwise miss out on some of your interest repayments if you exit the deal before the end of the agreement.

CASE STUDY

Paige is a keen cyclist and wants to buy a new bike. She has a part time job and her credit score shows that she will be able to get a loan, but she needs to look at her borrowing options. She researches online and finds a loan for £1,000 that looks suitable, but she needs to decide how long to borrow the money for.

Her options are shown below:

BORROWING	INTEREST RATE	INTEREST PAYABLE	TOTAL AMOUNT REPAYABLE	MONTHLY REPAYMENT
1 year loan	16.9% APR	£87.20	£1,087.20	£90.60 (12 months)
2 year loan	16.9% APR	£171.92	£1,171.92	£48.83 (24 months)
3 year loan	16.9% APR	£260.72	£1,260.72	£35.02 (36 months)

1. Which option should Paige choose? Why?

2. Think of three questions you would ask Paige before she takes out the loan.

3. What other borrowing options does Paige have?

4. Does Paige have to borrow the money? How else could she buy the bike?

CREDIT CARDS

The word "credit" can be a bit confusing as it has two meanings; an account "in credit" means that there is money in it that is available to spend. However, if you obtain goods or services "on credit" it means that you have borrowed the money to make the purchase.

Credit cards are available from most banks and allow you to purchase goods and services up to a certain limit. When you buy something with your credit card, the amount you spend is paid for by the credit card provider – it does not come out of your own account. The provider keeps a record of everything you have bought and every month you are sent a statement to show how much you have borrowed.

There are two ways of repaying a credit card. One of them charges you interest, but the other does not:

- Once you receive your monthly statement you repay the balance in full. You will not be charged any interest in this case.

- You pay off some of the statement balance. Credit cards require a minimum payment is made every month. This is around 3% of the balance or £5, whichever is greater. If you choose not to pay the balance in full then you will be charged interest on the remaining balance plus any further spending the following month.

DID YOU KNOW?

If you borrowed £3,000 on your credit card at 21 and only made the minimum repayments, you'll be almost 50 before it clears!

As with personal loans, potential customers will want to complete research and make comparisons to secure a good APR deal, and the credit card provider will carry out checks and investigate your credit history before approving the credit card. A good credit score will improve the chances of being given a credit card and generally mean lower interest rates and access to more deals.

The credit card provider will set a credit limit for your card – anything from a few hundred to several thousand pounds depending on your personal circumstances. You can then use the card to spend money up to that limit on whatever you want without seeking permission for each purchase. You can also have more than one credit card at a time – provided your credit rating is sufficiently strong.

Some companies offer low interest rates to new customers as a way of attracting their business. There may be a limited period where interest is 0% and this might also include "balance transfers" (debt transferred from another credit card or loan). After the introductory period, the interest rate may rise to a higher than normal level to compensate.

DID YOU KNOW?

Balance transfers allow you to take out a new card to pay off debt on old credit and store cards which are charging interest. The new card may have 0% interest or have a lower interest rate than you are currently paying, so you will become debt free quicker as the payments you make reduce the debt, rather than paying off the interest.

There are some positives to having a credit card:

- It is highly convenient when shopping and safer than carrying cash

- You can make instant purchases (up to your credit limit) though you should always be confident that you can repay the money

- Section 75 of the Consumer Credit Act 1974 means your credit card must protect purchases between £100 and £30,000 for free, so if there's a problem you could get your money back. If the firm you are dealing with goes bust or fails to deliver your purchase, you should get your money back from your credit provider. This applies even if you have only partly paid by credit card

- It is good for your credit score if you can show that you have borrowed money and paid it back as expected; this demonstrates financial responsibility

- Bonuses such as air miles, reward points and cashback may be a feature of a credit card.

DISCUSSION

Having looked at some positives about having a credit card, what do you think the possible negatives might be?

QUESTIONS:

1. How do both loan and credit card companies work out the specific interest a customer should pay?

2. What is a credit limit on a credit card?

3. Why is it important to understand the Terms and Conditions attached to borrowing money?

4. Why is it a good idea to pay off the balance on a credit card each month, if you can?

CASE STUDY

Nikita, Mackenzie, Jack, and Chika are a group of friends discussing their credit card interest rates. Nikita is a trainee chef earning £16,000 per year. She has only just been able to get a credit card because she missed a couple of payments on her mobile phone contract last year, so many providers refused her application. Her credit history isn't fantastic; therefore her credit card company gives her an APR of 30%.

Mackenzie is an IT software developer and has an excellent credit score, only using his credit card for big purchases like holidays and always paying his bill in full at the end of the month. His credit card company gives him an APR of 5%.

Jack is not very good with money. He has had loans in the past but has struggled to keep on top of the repayments. He has also had a credit card in the past but this was constantly "maxed out" to his credit limit. Only one credit card company were prepared to give him a credit card and they charge him a whopping APR of 50%.

Chika earns £30,000 as a graphic designer. She always pays off her credit card balance at the end of every month because she has set up a direct debit to make sure that she doesn't forget to pay her bill. Her card gives her an APR of 10%.

1. Why do you think individuals have different interest rates? Is this fair?

2. How could Nikita and Jack improve their credit score?

3. What advice would you give Nikita and Jack for the future?

 MORTGAGES

A mortgage is a long-term loan used to purchase property. On average, a home is the most expensive thing people buy in their lives. It is just not realistic to try and save up the amount of money required, so a mortgage is often used.

The term of a mortgage can vary, but most commonly it is 25 years. The cost of repaying the borrowing is spread over this term. The borrowing is secured against the property you have bought. This means that if you fail to make the repayments your home can be taken back by the lender and sold by them to recover their money – this is called repossession.

The interest rate on a mortgage is generally one of the lowest compared to other forms of borrowing. This is because of the long term and the fact that the loan is secured.

More information about mortgages can be found in the 'Further your knowledge' section.

 PAYDAY LENDERS

A payday lender is the name given to lenders who provide very short-term loans for relatively small amounts of money. As the name suggests, these are intended to cover any unexpected costs you might incur until you are able to repay the loan on your next payday.

Due to the very short-term nature of these types of loan, the interest rates can be very high – 1,500% APR is not unheard of. There are also penalties if the loan is not paid off when expected. Compared to other forms of flexible borrowing, like an arranged overdraft or a credit card, payday loans are very high cost.

One of the most controversial issues around payday loans is known as the "rollover". This is where someone is unable to pay off the loan at the end of the term (which could be as little as a week). In this case, the lender may suggest "rolling over" the loan for another week or more. While this may seem like a reasonable solution, it significantly increases the interest and charges you will pay.

Before applying for a payday loan consider all your other options, as they are likely to be much more costly.

CASE STUDY

Amelia works part time in a garden centre and has just moved into a one-bedroom flat where she lives alone. For the first 2 months, her wages only just covered the rent and bills that she needs to pay, but she needs to buy some new items of furniture as well. She takes on extra shifts at the garden centre and switches to buying supermarket own-brand food but still can't afford the furniture.

One evening, Amelia sees an advert on TV for a company called RapidLoan. It explains how easy it is to apply for a loan with them, and they won't even do a credit check to see if she can meet the repayments. The interest rate seems high, but she can get the money straightaway!

Amelia applies for the loan and the next day has an extra £300 in her bank account. She promises herself she will pay off the loan as soon as she gets paid at the end of the month.

She happily buys some new furniture but at the end of the month her gas and electricity bills are higher than expected and she can't pay off the loan in full and pay her bills too. She feels that her only option is to take out another loan on top of the one she already has, but she will definitely pay it all back at the end of the month.

Unfortunately, Amelia finds herself having to take out a new loan every month to try to clear the debt that has been building up, but because she needs more money for her day-to-day spending and to pay the interest on the loans, this simply isn't possible. After 4 months of this cycle, Amelia owes £1,500, which is more than she earns each month.

She can't believe how much she owes and how easy it was to end up in so much debt, it makes her worried and upset. She finally calls RapidLoan and tells them she is struggling, and they agree that she can repay the outstanding money over the next 6 months. However, they still send her emails regularly offering to lend her even more money, even though they know she can't afford it.

1. In your opinion, do you think that Amelia will be able to pay off her debts in 6 months? If so, why? If not, why not?

2. What impact do you think this experience has had on Amelia? How do you think she feels?

3. Is the payday lender acting responsibly? Explain your answer.

4. What advice would you offer Amelia?

5. In your opinion, what other borrowing options does Amelia have?

LOAN SHARKS

All of the borrowing we have discussed so far in this chapter is regulated by the Financial Conduct Authority (FCA). It is an organisation that is set by law to protect consumers, regulate companies and can fine them, or close them down, if they do not abide by the laws. It works to make sure that financial markets are honest, fair and effective so that consumers get a fair deal. If you felt you were not treated fairly you could always turn to the FCA as a last resort to help.

There are circumstances where individuals set themselves up as money lenders. These individuals are not regulated by the FCA, and their practise is illegal. As they are not regulated there is no limit to the interest rate they charge or the penalties they can apply.

Loan sharks tend to prey on the most vulnerable individuals, and those who struggle to be accepted for other forms of borrowing, such as those who have a poor credit history. There is a task force in England dedicated to investigating and prosecuting illegal money lenders – England Illegal Money Lending Team (IMLT).

 ## DID YOU KNOW?

Some loan sharks have attempted to charge interest rates as high as 719,000%. One woman who borrowed £500 ended up repaying £88,000. You might be harassed or threatened if you get behind with your repayments – there have been reports of people being intimidated or attacked. You might also be pressured into borrowing more money to repay one loan with another and end up in a spiral of debt that you can never repay.

 ## DID YOU KNOW?

Since 2004, the England IMLT have supported over 25,000 people and written off over £63,500,000 of debt.

 ## MANAGEABLE AND UNMANAGEABLE DEBT

Personal circumstances can change without warning, a borrower might suddenly find themselves unemployed and therefore not earning enough income to cover their debts and repayments. An unexpected family crisis may mean money intended for repaying debt has to be diverted elsewhere.

If debt is allowed to grow then it may start to become unmanageable; if action is not taken it can have serious financial consequences. In the same way, rushing into a substantial (or even unnecessary) purchase without proper thought, planning, budgeting or the means to repay, might also be seen as taking on unmanageable debt. Some people try to offset their debt by borrowing even more but this is no solution; a spiral effect can then ensue.

You spend more than you earn

You borrow to fill the gap

More of your income goes to repaying debts

You keep borrowing to maintain your lifestyle

The end result:

ALL YOUR INCOME GOES TOWARD REPAYING DEBT

YOU'VE NOTHING LEFT!

Source: moneysavingexpert.com

If you borrow to a level that is more than you have, or you anticipate having, then you may not have enough left to pay for what really matters and you could get into financial difficulty. The consequences of severe money difficulties can be:

- Financial (difficult to get further credit, legal proceedings)

- Emotional (stress, difficulties in relationships)

- Physical (illness brought on by stress)

- Spiritual (loss of self-esteem and the ability to cope).

This is why it is so important to make informed and manageable choices when dealing with your personal finances. Hopefully it will never happen, but if you do ever find yourself in a situation where debt has spiralled out of control, then there is help and advice available (you can find out more about this in the 'Risk and reward' chapter).

Talking about your circumstances to someone neutral and who can give impartial, considered advice can be of benefit, and this can include the financial organisation(s) involved. Many of them now recognise that they have a "duty of care" towards their customers and will help you to minimise difficulties and get yourself back on track with your finances. There are also a number of organisations and debt charities that you can turn to in times of need, such as Citizens Advice, StepChange and National Debtline.

QUESTIONS:

1. Give one example of a manageable debt and one example of an unmanageable debt.
2. Name two consequences of unmanageable debt.
3. What is probably the worst thing you can do if you get into debt?
4. Explain what you understand by the term "duty of care".

WHAT HAVE YOU LEARNT?

Using the knowledge you have gained from this chapter complete the activity below:

ACTIVITY

Carlo has an outstanding balance of £1,000 on his credit card but he urgently needs to replace his broken boiler. As he doesn't have any savings, and always ends the month overdrawn, he is considering taking out a payday loan to pay for this rather than using his credit card.

1. In your opinion, do you think that Carlo's credit card debt is manageable or unmanageable? Explain your reasons why.

2. Should Carlo take out the payday loan or use his credit card? Explain your answer.

3. What other borrowing options does Carlo have?

4. Recommend the most appropriate method of borrowing for Carlo and his situation.

5. Recommend to Carlo how he could reduce the balance on his credit card.

FURTHER
YOUR KNOWLEDGE

MORTGAGE BORROWING

Most people buying their own home will have a repayment mortgage. Monthly repayments are made, which go towards clearing some of the original loan, as well as paying some of the interest owed on it. There are three main types of repayment mortgage:

- **Fixed rate mortgage:**
  The interest rate is fixed for a specified number of years, so you will know exactly how much your monthly repayments will be during that time. If interest rates rise, you will reap the benefit as your repayments won't increase; you will, of course, lose out on any savings you could make if the rate goes down.

- **Variable rate mortgage:**
  The interest rate changes in line with the movement of interest rates so you could find yourself paying differing monthly amounts – sometimes less, sometimes more. This might be to your advantage but can make budgeting more difficult.

- **Tracker mortgage:**
  This tracks or moves in line with a declared interest rate (usually the Bank of England base rate).

The different interest rates charged will have a bearing on any decisions to be made about taking out a mortgage. In 2017, the average rates were: 1.99% (fixed), 4.23% (variable) and 2.34% (tracker).

To see how repayments are made, have a look at the following example. For a house costing £170,000 (the current UK average house price) you would typically need to find a 5% deposit (£8,500). The loan required would therefore be £161,500. If the mortgage term was 25 years and the interest rate was a fixed 1.99% then your schedule* might look like this:

YEAR	AMOUNT OF BORROWING REMAINING	INTEREST CHARGED	PRINCIPAL PAID	CLOSING BALANCE
1	£161,500.00	£3,168.08	£5,036.80	£156,463.20
5	£140,737.76	£2,751.13	£5,453.75	£135,284.01
10	£112,351.56	£2,181.07	£6,023.81	£106,327.75
15	£80,998.21	£1,551.39	£6,653.49	£74,344.72
20	£46,367.58	£855.93	£7,348.95	£39,018.63
25	£8,117.10	£87.75	£8,117.10	£0.00

Only selected years shown

The total interest to be paid on the loan will be **£43,621.23.**

1. Can you work out what is happening with the figures in the interest charged and principal paid columns and why?

2. Now calculate the monthly interest payment.

3. Use the figures to construct a graph or chart showing the relationship between principal paid, and interest charged, over the 25-year term of the mortgage.

HIGH COST CREDIT

There has been much concern in the worlds of economics and politics about issues surrounding high-cost credit and the effect it is having on society, particularly on those who might otherwise be financially excluded.

Read the text of a speech given by Andrew Bailey, chief executive of the Financial Conduct Authority in May 2018 about the impact of high cost credit. You can find it at: **www.fca.org.uk/news/speeches/high-cost-credit-what-next**

Create a list of 10 bullet points detailing the main points set out in the speech.

MAKING BORROWING CHOICES

Here are some borrowers with choices to make. Compare the deals they are considering by completing a table like the example shown for each. What would you advise in each case?

1. 19-year-old Toni wants £450 to purchase the latest high-end games console. It would take her much longer than she would like to save the money and the promotional sale she has spotted ends in a few days' time. As she has some money set aside, she is confident she can pay everything back within a year. Her options are:

a) Use her pre-arranged bank overdraft charged at 18% APR.

b) Apply for a loan from a credit union charging an APR of 12%.

c) Use her store card at an APR of 24%. With this she will get reward points to use on future purchases.

	MONTHLY REPAYMENT	TOTAL INTEREST	TOTAL COST OF LOAN
a			
b			
c			

d) Are there any other options which Toni might wish to consider?

2. Dane is a 25-year-old single parent of twins in desperate need of a new washer/dryer to keep up with the demand for clean clothes. This will cost £500. However, he is finding it difficult to make ends meet as it is; by cutting back and shopping wisely he can probably find £30 a month from his budget. His credit rating is likely to be low, but he has never checked, and assumes that his borrowing options will be extremely limited. His options are:

a) Buy via a catalogue across 36 months at an APR of 44.9%. There is a 12 month interest free, buy now, pay later option.

b) A 6 month payday loan where the APR is 750%.

c) A doorstep lender (loan shark) charging the equivalent of 1,200% APR for an 18 month loan; repayment is deferred for first 3 months.

	MONTHLY REPAYMENT	TOTAL INTEREST	TOTAL COST OF LOAN
a			
b			
c			

d) Are there any other options which Dane might wish to consider?

3. Faisal is 22 and works in an office as a trainee. Although he is currently on the National Minimum Wage, this will go up significantly when he becomes qualified. His one big indulgence in life is watching TV and, as this helps him to stay in and save money, he sees it as a good investment. He would like to get a new 4K Ultra HD model so wants to borrow £3,500 across approximately 3 years to help pay for it. He has calculated he can afford to pay back £110 per month. His options are:

a) Take out a 3 year hire purchase credit agreement from the dealership where he wants to buy the TV. The APR is 16.5%.

b) Get a bank loan (also 3 years). The APR is 9.75%.

c) Put the money required on his credit card. The APR is 15.9%.

	MONTHLY REPAYMENT	TOTAL INTEREST	TOTAL COST OF LOAN
a			
b			
c			

d) Are there any other options which Faisal might wish to consider?

MOVING ON FROM SCHOOL – THE WORLD OF WORK

WHAT ARE THE BIG FINANCIAL DECISIONS I'LL NEED TO MAKE?

In this chapter you'll explore some of the financial matters and decisions that you might face as you move on from full-time education.

These include understanding the ways that people get paid for work, the National Minimum Wage and National Living Wage, the financial implications of going to university, and making plans for when you retire from working.

> ## (!) DID YOU KNOW?
>
> **According to an Oxford University study, almost 50% of jobs existing today will be completely redundant in seven years.**

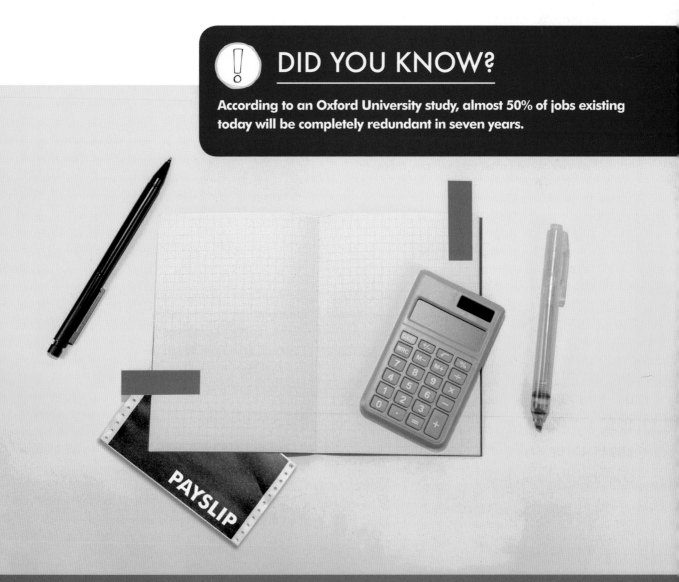

NEXT STEPS AFTER SCHOOL

When you leave school or college there are three main options available to you:

 ## 1. START AN APPRENTICESHIP

An apprenticeship combines practical training in a job with study. As an apprentice you will:

- Work alongside experienced staff

- Gain job-specific skills

- Earn a wage and get holiday pay

- Get time for study related to your role (usually one day a week).

Apprenticeships can take between 1 to 5 years to complete, depending on their level (there are intermediate, advanced, higher and degree level apprenticeships).

If you take an apprenticeship you will be paid for it. The minimum you'll get will be the National Minimum Wage for apprentices (which in 2018 was £3.70 per hour), however some employers will pay more.

You'll also be entitled to at least 20 days paid holiday per year, plus bank holidays.

 ## ACTIVITY

1. An average working week is 35 hours. What is the minimum an apprentice can earn per week?

2. Are there any costs you can think of which you might have to pay?

 ## 2. EMPLOYMENT

There is a wide range of work available for school and college leavers. For those going straight into work from school or college there is also a National Minimum Wage. This varies according to your age, and the rates change every April. For 2018 this was:

Under 18 – £4.20 per hour

18-20 – £5.90 per hour

21-24 – £7.38 per hour

Over 25 – £7.83 per hour

The National Minimum Wage is exactly that – it's the minimum an employer can pay. Employers can choose to pay more than this but must pay at least the National Minimum Wage for the age of person they employ. The amount paid by employers is determined by a number of factors, including:

- The level of responsibility within the role

- The skills required to do the role

- The level of experience they are looking for.

If you choose to work for yourself (be self-employed) then the minimum wage does not apply.

Ways you can be paid

There are a number of ways people are paid for the work that they do:

- **Salary** – A set amount of money paid once a month. This is based upon an agreed amount you would earn in one year.

- **Hourly rate** – You are paid a set amount for every hour you work. The more hours you do, the more you are paid. This is usually paid to you weekly or monthly.

- **Piece work** – You are paid a set amount for every unit you produce (e.g. picking a full punnet of raspberries). The more units you produce the more you are paid. This can be paid daily, weekly or monthly.

- **Commission** – Often linked to a salary in sales related jobs. For example, you may receive a share of the sales you make. This is paid in addition to a monthly salary.

You will explore even more ways you can be paid later on in the chapter.

The "gig" economy

The gig economy is a term that is used to describe the growing trend towards short-term contracts compared to permanent employment. Many people involved in this form of work are actually self-employed – they work for themselves rather than being directly employed by an organisation. Workers get paid for each "gig" they complete, for example providing courier services or delivering food.

Different types of employment contracts

There are a number of different ways that you can be employed in the UK. The most common ones include:

- **Full time** – Usually working 35 hours or more a week, full-time workers are provided with a contract of employment and receive benefits such as holiday pay, sick pay and pension opportunities.

- **Part time** – Usually works fewer hours than a full-time worker but receives the same treatment and benefits (though these may be proportionate to the number of hours worked per week).

- **Short term contract** – This can be on a full or part-time basis but is only for a fixed period of time.

- **Zero hours contracts** – These are casual contracts that offer no guarantee of any work. They often benefit employers who require staff at short notice to meet a temporary, or increased, need and can benefit employees as they may allow flexible working around other commitments. People on zero hours contracts are entitled to the National Minimum Wage and holiday pay, however with no guarantee of any work, and therefore income, zero hours contracts can make budgeting and planning your finances very difficult, as you don't know what you will receive in income from one month to the next.

 DID YOU KNOW?

According to the Department for Business, Energy and Industrial Strategy, 4.4% of the British population have worked in the gig economy – that's approximately 2.8 million people.

 ## ACTIVITY

1. How much would a 19-year-old on National Minimum Wage earn over a 35-hour week? What about a 28-year-old?

2. Calculate how much the two people above would earn in a year (hint: there are 52 weeks in a year).

 ## QUESTIONS

1. Which types of employment contracts provide the best protection for UK workers?

2. In your opinion, what are the benefits and implications of working in the gig economy?

 ## DID YOU KNOW?

Nearly a third of 18-year-olds in the UK go to university and by the age of 30, the percentage rises to nearly 50%.

Source: www.theguardian.com

 ## 3. GO TO UNIVERSITY

Most university courses last for 3 years, during which time you may be studying for a degree. There are costs associated with going to university, such as accommodation and living expenses, and for those going to university in England the cost of the course itself – called the tuition fee. Most students will take out a student loan to cover these costs. We'll find out a lot more about these later in the chapter, but student loans are a way of helping fund the costs of university and are then repaid according to your income once you get a job.

- For the 2018/19 year the maximum tuition fee is £9,250 per year.

- Living costs, such as accommodation, food, clothes, study books, travel and going out vary according to where in the country you go to university. A UK average cost is estimated to be around £230 per week.

Although there are costs associated with going to university, the hope for many students is that the qualification they leave with will enable them to enter the career of their choice and potentially at a higher income level.

 ## ACTIVITY

1. If an English university charged the maximum tuition fee for a 3-year degree, what would the total tuition fee be, based on the 2018/19 year?

2. An average university year is based on 40 weeks. How much is the average cost of living for a 3-year degree?

Student finance

We've seen that there are costs for those people who want to go to university, but there is also financial support in the form of student loans.

Student loans

If you decide to go to university you can apply to the Students Loans Company (SLC) for a Tuition Fees Loan. The SLC will pay the fees to the university directly.

In addition to a loan needed to pay the tuition fees, most students will also apply for a Maintenance Loan to cover their day-to-day living costs, like accommodation, food, transport, phone and laptop costs. The SLC will pay the Maintenance Loan directly to you.

You will then owe money to the SLC but you do not have to pay it back until you leave university, are in work and earning above a certain level. This applies to both the Tuition Fee Loan and Maintenance Loan.

The maximum you can borrow depends on how much your parents/carers earn (the household income) – for example, in the 2018/19 year this was £8,700 (£11,354 if studying in London). If the household income is about £25,000 you can expect to get the full loan each year, but as household income rises the Maintenance Loan is reduced. If household income is very high there is still a minimum Maintenance Loan given to students of about £3,000, so the student will be expected to make up this gap, likely to be with money from parents, as it is due to the parents/carers higher income that the student receives less.

The Maintenance Loan is split into three payments, which are paid directly into your bank account at the start of each term. So, unlike tuition fees, you are in control of how your maintenance loan is used.

If you did a 3-year university course, and borrowed the maximum Maintenance Loan each year, at the end of the course you would owe the SLC approximately:

£27,750 Tuition Fees Loan (3 x **£9,250**)
+
£26,100 Maintenance Loan (3 x **£8,700**)

£53,850 Total Loans

If you choose to do a 4-year course these figures would increase.

This sounds like a lot of debt, but it is very important to have the full picture about when and how much you will have to repay:

1. **You only start to repay any loans once you have got your degree, left university and got a job earning over a certain amount.**

2. **You only repay when, or for as long as, you earn more than £25,000 per year.**

   You repay 9% of anything you earn over £25,000. So, if you earn £30,000 a year you would pay back 9% of £5,000. That's £450 in a year. If your income drops below £25,000 your repayments will stop and only re-start again once you earn above £25,000.

   Note that the earnings threshold does tend to increase each year, making the amount you are able to earn before you start making repayments slightly higher. This accounts for the impact of inflation – the increasing cost of goods and services from one year to the next.

3. **After 30 years, all remaining debt is wiped.**

   If you still owe any money on your student loan after 30 years (from the April after graduation) the debt is cancelled. If you never get a job earning over the threshold, it means you won't have repaid a penny. If you still owe £20,000 after 30 years the debt is cancelled, and you owe nothing.

4. **The loan repayments are made automatically.**

   All student loans since 1998 have been repaid through the payroll – this means that once you're working, your employer will deduct the repayments from your salary before you get it (we'll look at this more a little later on). The amount you receive in your bank account each month already has it removed. So, you don't have to worry about organising how to pay the debt – it will be paid automatically.

5. Student loans DO NOT go on credit files.

When you borrow from a bank for a credit card, loan or mortgage, lenders look at three pieces of information before they decide whether or not to give you the loan: your application form; any previous dealings they've had with you; and crucially, the information on your credit reference files.

Your credit history will be listed on these files – but student loans are not included. This means the money you owe on a student loan will not impact your credit worthiness.

Interest on student loans

As with other forms of borrowing, interest is also applied to student loans and will be taken into account when your repayments are calculated. To find out more about the impact of interest on borrowing, take a look at the 'Borrowing' chapter.

DID YOU KNOW?

The way student loans work is different in England, Scotland, Wales and Northern Ireland.

This information is for an English student attending an English University.

DISCUSSION

Because of the way student loans are repaid there is an argument that they are more like a graduate tax than a loan repayment. What do you think?

CASE STUDY

Syrah is a first-year student on a 3-year degree course. After 3 weeks of her course she has noticed that her maintenance loan is being spent faster than she had expected. Her parents' income allowed her to receive the full maintenance loan and at the start of term she had £2,880 paid into her bank account. The first term lasts for 12 weeks.

As it's her first year, Syrah lives in a hall of residence. The cost of this was £1,440 for the term, which had to be paid in the first week. She has looked at all of her expenses to date and worked out that after 3 weeks she has spent the following:

Food and drink	**£120**
Clothes	**£60**
Transport	**£54**
Mobile phone	**£36**
Laundry	**£30**
Books	**£60**
Socialising	**£105**
Insurance	**£36**
Gym membership	**£6**
Total spending over 3 weeks is	**£507**

To help Syrah keep track of her spending, prepare a weekly budget for her.

What advice would you give to Syrah to help manage her money?

STUDENT BURSARIES, GRANTS AND SCHOLARSHIPS

In addition to the student loans that are available from SLC it is very important to explore other possible sources of income.

Many universities offer bursaries, which are usually cash awards – e.g. £1,000. These do not need to be repaid and are available to help students whose household has a low level of income.

A scholarship is also often a cash award, this time given to students who do particularly well in their exams preceding university or college. The scholarship may be awarded by the university or a company and may pay the tuition fees for a course in full or in part.

Some universities also offer grants. This again is a cash award that you do not have to repay. It is usually given for a very specific purpose, like studying abroad or undertaking research that costs a bit of money.

If you are a student with a learning difficulty, health problem or disability you may also be entitled to claim for Disabled Students' Allowance to cover some of the extra costs to support your additional needs. This does not have to be repaid.

There are also certain degree courses that attract specific bursaries, grants and scholarships because the economy needs more people to qualify from them. A good example is if you wanted to become a maths teacher – there is extra funding because there is a shortage of maths teachers.

All of this extra funding has to be applied for, so it is really important for potential students to carry out research and make sure they are not missing out on money that could help them while at college or university.

There is also the option of taking on part-time work while at university to generate extra income, however you would need to ensure that this doesn't affect your studies.

EARNINGS

Whether you go straight into work from school, follow an apprenticeship, or go to university, you'll expect to earn some money for the job you end up doing.

It may sound simple to work out exactly how much you will be paid for the work you do, but it's not always as straightforward as you think. There are a number of things which are taken off the amount you earn before you receive it – you don't always get to take home everything you earn. These are called deductions. The main deductions you will come across will be:

- Income Tax – tax based on your earnings

- National Insurance – tax on earnings to help pay for state benefits such as state pension and sick pay

- Pension contribution – often paid by both the employer and employee to build up a pension pot for when you retire

- Student loan repayment – paying back the money you borrowed (plus interest), but only if you earn over the threshold.

When you receive your pay from your job, you'll most probably also receive a payslip. This piece of paper contains information about you and your earnings. Your payslip will also show all of your deductions.

! DID YOU KNOW?

According to official UK government data, £185 billion was collected from Income Tax payments in 2017, an increase of £8 billion from the year before.

Look at the payslip for Sam Green who is a senior stylist in a national chain of hairdressers.

DATE	EMPLOYER		EMPLOYEE	
30/06/2018	Brushes Hair Salon		S Green	
DEPARTMENT	**N.I. NUMBER**	**TAX CODE**	**PAY METHOD**	**PERIOD**
Hairdressing	YX542789	1185L	BACS	Month 3
DESCRIPTION	**UNITS DUE**	**DEDUCTIONS**	**TOTALS TO DATE**	
Basic Pay		Tax **117.60** N.I **110.76** Pension **48.75**	Total Gross Pay	**4,875.00**
			Taxable Pay	**1,912.50**
			Tax Paid	**352.80**
			Employee NI	**332.28**
			Employer NI	**382.11**
			Employee Pension	**146.25**
			Employer Pension	**97.50**
HOURS	**GROSS PAY**	**DEDUCTIONS**	**NET PAY**	
Standard 35 hours per week	1,625.00	277.11	1,347.89	

DISCUSSION

Before reading more about payslips, what do you know already?

- What is the tax called that you can see on the payslip in deductions?
- What does NI stand for?
- Why is this Month 3?
- What is the significance of the numbers in the tax code?
- What is Sam's take-home pay?

 # PAYSLIPS EXPLAINED

Deductions

On the payslip you can see that amounts for Income Tax, National Insurance contributions, and pension will be deducted from your gross pay. These are called compulsory deductions because you must pay them.

People who borrowed money to go to university and earn over the income threshold may also have student loan repayments taken off their gross pay.

Income Tax

Everyone is allowed to earn some money before they start to pay Income Tax.

This is your Personal Tax Allowance. It is set by the government each year, for example in 2018/19 this is £11,850 per year for most people. The income that you earn above your personal tax allowance is called your taxable income.

Once your income goes above this allowance you will pay Income Tax.

It will start at **20%** On anything you earn above **£11,850** up to **£46,350**	Any annual income above **£46,350** is taxed at **40%** up to **£150,000**	Any annual income over **£150,000** is taxed at **45%**

This means that for those on the lowest income they pay no Income Tax at all, but the more you earn the higher the amount of Income Tax you pay (although the more you earn the more you take home too!).

Charging different rates of tax at different levels of income is known as tax banding.

You can find updated allowances and tax rates at **www.gov.uk**

Worked examples

We will assume the following 2018/19 figures:

Personal Tax Allowance – **£11,850**

Basic Tax Rate – **20%** on your first **£34,500** of taxable income (from **£11,850** to **£46,350**)

Higher Tax Rate – **40%** on taxable income of **£34,500** to **£150,000**

1 A cleaner who earns £15,000 per year – how much Income Tax do they pay?

The cleaner pays £630 Income Tax per year (just over £50 per month). This is 4.2% of their income.

Income (£)	Tax rate (%)	Tax paid (£)
11,850	0	0
3,150	20	630
Total 15,000		**630**

2 A lorry driver who earns £30,000 per year – how much Income Tax do they pay?

The lorry driver pays £3,630 in Income Tax per year (just over £300 per month). This is 12.1% of their income.

Income (£)	Tax rate (%)	Tax paid (£)
11,850	0	0
18,150	20	3,630
Total 30,000		**3,630**

3 A software developer earns £70,000 per year – how much Income Tax do they pay?

The software developer pays £16,360 in Income Tax per year (just over £1,360 per month). This is 23.37% of their income.

Income (£)	Tax rate (%)	Tax paid (£)
11,850	0	0
34,500	20	6,900
23,650	40	9,460
Total 70,000		**16,360**

In this last example, you can see that the person is paying some of their income at the higher tax rate. Notice that it is only **some** of their income and not all of it that is taxed at the higher rate of 40%, and they are still entitled to the personal tax allowance.

QUESTIONS

1. What do you call the amount you are allowed to earn before you begin paying tax on your earnings?

2. How does tax banding attempt to ensure a fair tax system?

3. What is meant by the term "deductions" on a payslip?

Tax Code

Your Tax Code will show how much income you are allowed to earn before you start to pay Income Tax – your personal tax allowance. It is the first 4 numbers of your tax allowance followed by a letter. Most people have the letter "L", which indicates that they have the basic tax allowance.

It is your responsibility to check that the tax code on your payslip is correct. If it's not, you could be paying too much tax and need to get a rebate (a refund of your overpayment). Or, you could be paying too little and will need to get in contact with HM Revenue and Customs (HMRC) to correct it. This can happen to students who take on part-time work, so be careful to check your tax code, and if you think you're paying too much Income Tax contact HMRC.

Anyone of working age, whether they are an employee or self-employed, can track and manage their tax and National Insurance contributions using the Government Gateway online portal.

ACTIVITY

Work out how much tax would be paid by:

1. A part-time librarian earning £11,000 per year.

2. An engineer earning £55,000 per year.

3. A professional diver earning £83,000 per year.

DID YOU KNOW?

If you add a zero to the numbers in your tax code it will tell you how much you are allowed to earn before paying Income Tax. For example, if you code is 1185L, your personal tax allowance will be £11,850

National Insurance

Everyone receives their National Insurance number just before their 16th birthday. It will stay with you for life. Most people who work have to pay National Insurance contributions.

National Insurance is paid at approximately 12% of your income. In 2018/19 there is a lower earnings limit of £8,424, below which you pay no National Insurance at all. There is also an upper threshold of £46,350, above which you only pay 2% of your income.

National Insurance contributions help to build up your entitlement to certain benefits, such as state pension, maternity allowance and financial support if you are unable to work.

In addition to employees paying National Insurance, it must also be paid by your employer for every worker they employ. If you look at the sample payslip you can see that the amounts are similar, but the employer pays slightly more per month.

Worked examples

How much National Insurance would the following pay?

a) A newly-qualified nurse earning £23,000 per year

Answer – On the first £8,424 of their salary National Insurance is £0

They pay 12% on the remaining £14,576 of their salary

= £1,749 per year (or £146 per month)

They do not earn enough to reach the upper threshold

b) A lawyer earning £60,000 per year

Answer – On the first £8,424 of their salary National Insurance is £0

They pay 12% on the next £37,926 of their salary = £4,551 per year

They pay 2% on the final £13,650 of their salary = £273 per year

So, in total, the lawyer pays £4,551 +£273 = **£4,824 per year (or £402 per month)**

Gross pay

The total income that you receive before any deductions are made is called your gross pay. Gross pay will always be bigger than net pay.

In the sample payslip, Sam received basic pay after working for a standard 37.5 hour week. Other amounts are sometimes added to the basic pay. For example, if you work longer hours than the standard week you might earn overtime pay. Also, if you successfully meet some targets set for you, you could earn a bonus.

 ACTIVITY

Calculate how much National Insurance you would pay if you earned:

- £10,000 per year.

- £30,000 per year.

- £100,000 per year.

Net pay

This is the pay you have left after your deductions have been removed. It is sometimes called your take-home pay. All the deductions are made before you receive the money so that you do not have to do anything about it. This system is called Pay As You Earn (PAYE).

Total deductions

This sums up all the deductions taken from your pay. On the sample payslip you can see the Total Tax Paid, Total Employee NI and Total Employee Pension.

If you were to leave the organisation that is paying you, then you should receive a P45 form. This would contain:

- Your leaving date.

- How much tax you have paid so far in this tax year.

How much pay you had earned so far in this tax year.

A UK tax year runs from 6 April to the following 5 April. So, this payslip for June is month 3. At the end of the tax year your employer should give you a P60 form which will tell you:

- The **total amount of tax** you have paid in the tax year.

- The **total amount of pay** you have earned in the tax year.

Other deductions from your payslip

Pension scheme contributions:

- Many people contribute to a pension scheme (a different one from the state pension that you qualify for by making National Insurance contributions)

- These pension contributions are taken from your gross pay. Importantly, pension contributions are taken off your gross pay before Income Tax is calculated. This means the pension contributions result in you paying less Income Tax

- If you pay tax at the 20% rate this means that for every £10 you put into your pension, you are making a further tax saving of £2 in Income Tax.

Voluntary deductions:

- Some people also make payments to a charity or save into a credit union account.

QUESTIONS

1. Explain the difference between gross pay and net pay.

2. Name three deductions you might see on a payslip.

3. What does the term PAYE mean?

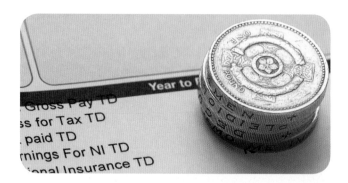

 DID YOU KNOW?

More people than ever are setting up their own business and according to the Office of National Statistics, 4.8 million people (15.1% of the labour workforce) were self-employed in 2017, compared to 3.3 million (12% of labour workforce) in 2001.

SELF-EMPLOYED

A person is self-employed if they run a business for themselves and take responsibility for its successes and failures. They may also be an independent contractor who provides a service for an organisation when the business does not have the staff to provide this themselves. Self-employed people have the flexibility to choose when they work, and how much work to take on, however they do not benefit from many of the rights that employees have, such as holiday pay or sick pay.

For people who are self-employed the same tax bands apply, but they only pay tax on their profits:

Business income – Business expenses = Profit

- Business income is the money you are paid by your customers. For example, the business income of a window cleaner is all of the money paid to them by customers for cleaning their windows over the year

- Business expenses are the costs that you incur in order to run your business. For the window cleaner, this might be the cost of running a van and the materials needed to clean the windows.

Once the profit has been worked out, it is taxed using the same tax bands we have seen before.

People who are self-employed also pay National Insurance through their Self-Assessment Tax Return. In 2018/19 there are two types to pay:

Class 2 National Insurance – a fixed rate of £2.95 per week if your profits are above £6,205 plus;

Class 4 National Insurance – based on the business profits below

Business Profit	National Insurance
Up to £8,424	0%
£8,424 - £46,350	9%
Over £46,350	2%

People who are employed will have their tax deducted each month before they receive their income and are able to see the Income Tax they have paid on their payslip. Those who are self-employed have to complete a Self-Assessment Tax Return once a year. They tell the government what their business income and expenses are and it calculates the tax they are required to pay.

BEWARE – It can be a lot harder to make sure you have put aside enough to pay your tax bill as a self-employed person as you only make one or two payments per year. The rule of thumb is to put aside 30% of everything you earn to make sure there is enough to pay the tax owed.

Worked examples

How much National Insurance would the following pay?

a) A self-employed gardener earning an annual profit of £22,500

Answer – Class 2 National Insurance –
£2.95 x 52 (weeks in a year)
= £153.40
Plus, Class 4 National Insurance – on first £8,424 of profits, National Insurance is £0
Then pay 9% on remaining £14,076 of profits
= £1,267
They do not earn enough profit to pay the upper threshold
Total National Insurance = £153.40 + £1,267
= £1,420.40

ACTIVITY

1. Work out how much tax would be paid by a self-employed electrician earning a profit of £28,00 per year.

2. Calculate how much National Insurance a self-employed gardener with £48,000 profit per year would pay.

THE WORLD OF WORK

METHODS OF PAYMENT

When you enter employment, you may well be paid in a variety of ways. Here is a list of some of the methods of payment with a brief explanation.

Wages: Earnings paid on an hourly basis.

Salary: Earnings paid monthly into a bank or building society account. In many jobs you would not be entitled to get overtime as you would be expected to put in extra hours when required.

Commission: Payment based on the value of sales you make. Sometimes you get it in addition to a basic salary.

Piecework: Payment for each item you produce. The more you produce, the more pay you will get.

Fees: A one-off payment for a professional service.

Bonus: An additional payment for working hard or hitting targets.

Overtime: When you work longer hours than is in your contract you can volunteer to work longer (overtime) usually at a better rate than normal e.g. "double-time".

Shift payment: This is paid for working unusual hours, for example, during the night. It would be in addition to your normal pay.

Minimum Wage: An hourly rate that your employer cannot drop below. See previous section on NMW and NLW.

CASE STUDY

Spot the difference

Alba and Tyrell are both plumbers. Alba has been self-employed for 3 years and gets her business largely through word of mouth. She charges £30 per hour for her labour and at the moment has no problem finding work; some of her customers have even been waiting for 2 months for her to be able to work for them. Alba loves watching live music and really likes the flexibility of working for herself so that when she wants to she can finish early. Or, she can take a day off at short notice if she has to travel far to a gig. She very rarely works at the weekend.

Tyrell is employed by a large company. He gets a salary of £30,000 per year and is entitled to 32 days holiday per year plus bank holidays. He works a 40-hour week but is often given the chance to work overtime at double pay. Most of his work is maintaining existing properties that are run by housing associations. Tyrell also has to regularly work a night shift at weekends, which means he often cannot play football – his main interest outside work. Tyrell enjoys the security of a regular salary but knows he might earn more if he was self-employed.

DISCUSSION

Can you spot five differences between Alba and Tyrell's jobs?

WHY DO WE PAY INCOME TAX?

CASE STUDY

Tom works in sales; the company he works for pay him a basic salary of £15,000 per year, plus 5% of the value of any sales that he makes. Last year he made £500,000 in sales. Next year, his target is £800,000 in sales and if he meets the target he gets the same 5% bonus on top of his basic salary.

Lisa also works in sales, but she is on a salary of £52,000 per year with no commission. If her sales rise or fall her salary stays the same.

Who do you think has the best pay deal, Tom or Lisa? Explain your choice.

What is the history of Income Tax and why do we pay it?

Income Tax was introduced by William Pitt the Younger more than 200 years ago when he needed the money to pay for the wars against Napoleon, the leader of France. For many years, Income Tax was only paid by the very rich, but in the 20th century it began to rise and, by 1930, 10 million people were paying Income Tax. The rates rose again to pay for the Second World War and, in 1944, the system of Pay As You Earn (PAYE) was introduced.

Today, Income Tax is the biggest individual source of income for the government and accounts for nearly 25% of government income. This, together with the income the government raises from other sources, is used to pay for all the various areas of government spending.

Examples of government spending include:

- Provision of State Pensions, low income support and Jobseeker's Allowance
- The National Health Service (NHS) – building hospitals, providing treatment and paying doctors and nurses
- Spending on schools, colleges and universities
- The Armed Forces – keeping the Army, Navy and Royal Air Force up to date with the latest technology, and paying the salaries of our military personnel
- Local councils – providing services such as emptying your rubbish bins, cleaning the streets, etc.

All of these services, and many more, are paid for by the government and to do so they must use the income that they receive from taxation. Not just Income Tax but also National Insurance, Value Added Tax (VAT), Council Tax, taxes on business profits, vehicle tax, and taxes on alcohol, cigarettes, etc.

 DID YOU KNOW?

Income Tax and National Insurance are both collected by HM Revenue and Customs. Income Tax is used to help provide funding for public services such as education and the welfare system, while National Insurance contributions are used to build up an individual's entitlement to state benefits such as the state pension.

ACTIVITY

What happens to our taxes?

The table below shows the money that was raised in the UK through taxation for 2016/17. As you can see, there are different ways the government collects taxation from individuals and businesses.

PUBLIC SECTOR REVENUE 2016/2017	£BILLION
Income Tax	£182
National Insurance	£126
Excise duties	£48
Corporation tax	£43
VAT	£138
Business Rates	£28
Council tax	£30
Other (taxes)	£69
Other (non-taxes)	£51
TOTAL	**£715**

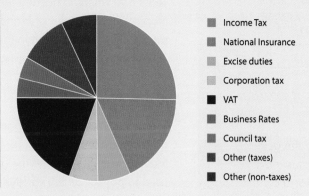

- Income Tax
- National Insurance
- Excise duties
- Corporation tax
- VAT
- Business Rates
- Council tax
- Other (taxes)
- Other (non-taxes)

1. Identify which taxes may affect you in the future.

2. What effects will these have on you? Think about positives and negatives.

The next table shows how this revenue was spent by the government in 2016/17

UK GOVERNMENT SPENDING 2016/17	£BILLION
Debt interest	£39
Other (inc. EU spending)	£49
Public order and safety	£34
Housing and environment	£34
Industry, agriculture and employment	£24
Defence	£46
Education	£102
Transport	£29
Social protection	£240
Social services	£30
Health	£145
TOTAL	**£772**

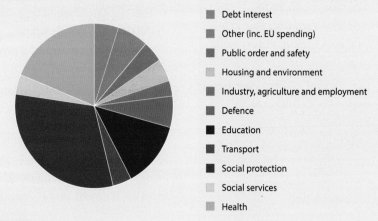

- Debt interest
- Other (inc. EU spending)
- Public order and safety
- Housing and environment
- Industry, agriculture and employment
- Defence
- Education
- Transport
- Social protection
- Social services
- Health

Source: Office for Budget Responsibility 2016/17

3. Which parts of the public sector receive the most funding?

4. By looking at the totals it is clear to see that the government spends more than it raises in tax. Is this a problem?

5. In your opinion, do you think tax is a good thing?

PENSIONS

A pension is a specific type of long-term savings plan that you build up during your working life to fund your retirement (when you stop working in later life). It is intended to provide money for people to live on once they no longer receive an income from work.

Most people will pay into a pension scheme and these payments will appear on your payslip in the deductions section. Putting money into a pension scheme is like having a savings account, but unlike normal savings you cannot use your money until you reach retirement age.

There are two main types of pension:

 ## 1. THE STATE PENSION

This is paid by the government. To qualify for the state pension, you must have paid National Insurance (NI) contributions for a certain number of years.

The number of years you have paid National Insurance contributions will affect the amount of state pension that you receive. To qualify for the maximum state pension, you would need to pay NI contributions for a minimum of 35 years. This would mean you would currently receive approximately £165 per week (2018) from your state retirement age.

The state retirement age has changed in recent years, but for most people it will eventually be 68 for both men and women. However, this age is regularly reviewed by the government as advances in healthcare enable people to work and live longer.

 ## 2. WORKPLACE PENSIONS

These are set up by your employer. You will pay a percentage of your monthly income into the pension. This is taken off your gross income before it is taxed. This means your pension contribution is tax free.

Another huge benefit of a workplace pension is that your employer will also contribute to it. This is additional to your income and is also tax free.

The money paid in by you and/or your employer is put into investments (see the 'Risk and reward' chapter) by your pension provider. The amount you get when you come to withdraw from your pension depends on how much was paid in and how well the investments have done.

The pension provider is the company or organisation that looks after your pension for you. They may be chosen for you by your employer, or you may be able to choose your own. It is very important to know who your pension provider is and what they intend to do with your money as the value of your pension pot can go up or down depending on your investments.

AUTOMATIC ENROLMENT INTO WORKPLACE PENSIONS

Since February 2018 all existing and new employers must automatically enrol any eligible members of staff into a workplace pension scheme. This means the vast majority of people will start a pension from the beginning of their working life.

Auto-enrolment applies to employees between the age of 22 and their state retirement age, who earn over £10,000 a year and work in the UK.

There are minimum amounts that must be contributed, and by 2019 the employee must contribute a minimum of 5% of their pay and the employer must contribute a minimum of 3%. Both employees and employers can decide how much to contribute to the pension scheme, the more that goes in, the bigger the amount of money there will be when the worker retires.

Along with the state pension, self-employed individuals can also set up their own private pension with a pension provider. These operate similarly to workplace pensions but obviously there is no employer to choose a scheme for you and no employer contributions.

People may also choose other ways of building up a retirement fund, for example by investing in a stocks and shares ISA or property. But remember that anyone opting out of a workplace pension scheme would lose their employer's contributions.

ACTIVITY

Key facts about the ageing population in the UK:

- In 1901, the life expectancy for women was 45, and 49 for men

- In 1961, the life expectancy for women was 76, and 71 for men

- In 1998, the life expectancy for women was 80, and 75 for men

- In 2017, the life expectancy for women was 83, and 79 for men.

Using the above figures:

1. What trends are occurring in life expectancy in the UK?

2. What do you think is happening to the proportion of someone's life which is spent working?

3. What are the **financial** implications of these trends for each of the groups below:
   - The government
   - People who are still working
   - People who are retired.

QUESTIONS

1. Explain the difference between the state pension and a workplace pension scheme.

2. What is the benefit to younger people of auto enrolment?

CASE STUDY

The average pensioner in the UK

In 2017, a typical pensioner needed a minimum annual income of approximately £10,850 in order to cover basic living costs, the breakdown was as follows:

£1,600   Recreation and culture (TV subscriptions and equipment, hobbies, etc.)

£1,550   Food and non-alcoholic drink

£1,500   Housing, fuel and power (rent and maintenance, but not mortgages)

£1,250   Transport (rail fares, cars, etc.)

£850   Household goods and services (furniture, appliances, etc.)

£800   Restaurants and hotels

£400   Clothing and footwear

£250   Alcohol and tobacco

£200   Health

£350   Communication (phones, stamps, broadband, etc.)

£850   Miscellaneous goods and services (personal care, insurance, bank charges, etc.)

£1,250   Other expenditure items (mortgages, council tax, interest on credit cards, payments to children, etc.)

Total: £10,850

Using the information above and what you know about the size of the state pension, what advice would you give to someone planning for their retirement?

Source: Adapted from research by Key Retirement based on family spending data from the Office for National Statistics.

HELP FOR PEOPLE ON LOW INCOMES

THE NATIONAL MINIMUM WAGE AND NATIONAL LIVING WAGE

In the UK, a National Minimum Wage was created by the National Minimum Wage Act 1998. It was introduced to prevent workers under the age of 25 on low pay being exploited by employers.

In 2016, the Act was amended, and a National Living Wage was introduced for workers who are 25 and over.

The rates for both the National Minimum Wage (NMW) and National Living Wage (NLW) are reviewed each year. In 2018, the NMW for an 18 year old was nearly £6 per hour and the NLW was nearly £8 per hour.

In addition to these laws, over 3,500 employers are also committed to paying the UK Voluntary Living Wage Rate, which is set by the Living Wage Foundation campaign group. This is independently calculated and designed to reflect the "real cost of living in the UK and London". It tends to be higher than the NLW but is not enforceable by law.

WELFARE SYSTEM

In the section on the history of Income Tax and why we pay it, we saw that some of the Income Tax collected by the government is used to support those on low levels of income.

People on low incomes, or people who have no income, may be entitled to claim benefits to help them pay for essential living expenses. Since 2013, a new system has gradually been introduced called Universal Credit.

Universal Credit replaces a range of benefits such as Income Support, Housing Support, Working Tax Credit and Child Tax Credit. Therefore, people entitled to claim Universal Credit will receive one type of support. If your income goes up because you can work more or earn more, the intention is that the level of Universal Credit will gradually reduce.

ACTIVITY

Find out what the current rates are for the NMW, NLW and UK Voluntary Living Wage.

In pairs or small groups, discuss why you think the government has not made the NLW the same as the Voluntary Living Wage.

WHAT HAVE YOU LEARNT?

Using the knowledge you have gained from this chapter, complete the activity and case study below:

ACTIVITY

Create an online blog (or film a vlog) for a young person who has recently got their first full-time job.

Summarise:

- The deductions that will be made from their income

- Where these deductions go and how they are then spent.

CASE STUDY

Daisy is 18 and has recently left school to pursue a career in jewellery design. She is unsure about which career direction to take and is looking at the following options:

a) Study a degree in Jewellery Design

b) Undertake an advanced apprenticeship in Art and Design

c) Find a job in jewellery design

d) Set up her own jewellery design business

1. What financial considerations would Daisy need to make for each option?

2. Discuss the financial benefits and risks of each option.

3. In your opinion, what advice would you give to Daisy?

FURTHER
YOUR KNOWLEDGE

TAX BANDS

Jamie graduated in Digital Media and got her first full-time job as a social media assistant working for a leading leisure company. Her starting salary was £25,350 per year, and for the next 3 years she received an annual pay rise of £3,250. Recently she has been promoted to social media manager and has received a further pay increase of £8,875.

1. Based on 2018/2019 tax bands, how much Income Tax will she pay?

2. How much does Jamie have left after Income Tax has been deducted?

3. What proportion (%) of her current salary is Income Tax?

Last month, Jamie performed really well, and her boss rewarded her with a one-off bonus of £5,000 paid through her salary.

4. Again, based on 2018/19 tax bands, how much Income Tax will Jamie pay now?

5. What proportion (%) of her salary is now Income Tax?

6. As a result of the bonus payment, how much extra tax will she pay?

7. In pairs, discuss what impact this bonus will have on her income?

PENSION CONTRIBUTIONS

Question 1

Hebron has been automatically enrolled into his employer's workplace pension scheme, and has decided not to opt out of the scheme. His employer, JW Garden Design Ltd, has issued the following information to staff about how much they intend to contribute and how much the employees will be expected to contribute per year. Both contributions are worked out as a percentage of each employee's basic salary.

EMPLOYER PAYS	EMPLOYEES PAY	TOTAL CONTRIBUTION
3%	5%	8%

If Hebron earned £18,000 per year his employer would contribute £540 per year (£45 per month) and he would contribute £900 per year (£75 per month).

a) Imagine Hebron's salary is £24,000 and, using the data above, calculate the pension contributions that would be made by Hebron and his employer.

Hebron's employer plans on increasing the pension contributions in 2020, these are:

EMPLOYER PAYS	EMPLOYEES PAY	TOTAL CONTRIBUTION
6%	8%	14%

b) If his salary remains the same, calculate the pension contributions that would be made by Hebron and his employer.

c) Does this increase in contributions mean he will receive a larger pension when he retires? Explain your answer.

Question 2

Many public-sector pension employee contribution rates are staggered so that those on the lowest salaries pay the least amount and those who earn the most, pay more. The following information shows the pension contributions made in the Fire Service if a firefighter joined the pension scheme after 2015.

Employee contribution rates

PENSIONABLE PAY	FIREFIGHTERS' PENSION SCHEME (2015)
Up to £27,818	11.0%
£27,819–£51,515	12.9%
£51,516–£142,500	13.5%
£142,501 or more	14.5%

Employer contribution rates – 14.3%

Source: Firefighters' Pensions England

1. Calculate the employee and employer contributions per year if a firefighter earned a salary of

   a) £16,120

   b) £32,500

   c) £68,750

b) In pairs, look at the range of employee contributions for firefighters in the table above. In your opinion do you think these are fair? Justify your answer.

SELF-EMPLOYMENT

Self-employed people pay Income Tax on their business's profits, rather than the total amount of income earned. To calculate profit, the business owner must subtract the business expenses from the business income. The formula for profit is:

Income – Expenses = Profit or Loss

For example, if a business sold 10 pens for £2 each the income would be £20. If it cost the business owner £8 to buy the pens, the business profits would be £12. Because there is no employer to take the Income Tax, self-employed people must submit a self-assessment form every year to HMRC. The business owner will indicate on their self-assessment form how much income they earned during the 12-month period and how much they spent on expenses. Whatever the difference, will be the amount that is taxed.

For example, Amira earned £29,362 as a self-employed caterer providing food for private parties during the last tax year and spent £16,019 on expenses (ingredients, utensils, etc.). This means she made £13,343 profit.

£29,362 - £16,019 = £13,343 profit

Just like employees, Amira also gets a personal tax allowance of £11,850 so she will only pay tax on the remaining £1,493. This will be charged at 20% so her tax bill will be £298.60.

PROFIT (£)	TAX RATE (%)	TAX PAID (£)
11,850	0	0
1,493	20	298.60

THE WORLD OF WORK
FURTHER YOUR KNOWLEDGE

When it comes to paying Income Tax on business profits, the same tax bands apply as those of an employee.

Alba, the self-employed plumber, has calculated the number of hours she has worked for each of the past 6 months and how much she spent on expenses (supplies, petrol, phone bills, etc).

MONTH	HOURS WORKED	INCOME (£30 PER HOUR)	EXPENSES (£)	PROFIT/LOSS
April	168		927	
May	195		1,621	
June	110		782	
July	72		437	
August	46		210	
September	197		2,932	
TOTAL				

a) Complete the table above and calculate Alba's profit over these 6 months

b) Calculate her Income Tax payment for the 6 months from April to September

RISK AND REWARD
WHY DO SOME PEOPLE TAKE RISKS WITH MONEY?

In this chapter you will explore what is meant by financial risk and reward.

You will think about the financial decisions you could be faced with, and the level of risk involved in these.

You'll explore the reasons that people take risks with money, and the link between risk and reward.

You will also find out how you can protect yourself against financial risks and where you can go to get help if the risk you have taken turns out to be a bad decision.

! DID YOU KNOW?

Risk taking causes changes in the brain as it releases adrenaline, causing an intense feeling of pleasure. This is why some risk taking, like gambling, can become addictive.

TYPES OF PERSONAL FINANCIAL RISK

In order to gain financial rewards, there is often some element of risk involved – the outcome of a financial decision may not be certain or guaranteed. There could be the possibility of a significant financial gain, but there could also be the risk of no gain or even a loss, leaving you worse off than when you started.

There are a number of different types of personal financial risks, these include:

RISKS ASSOCIATED WITH YOUR INCOME

For most people, their most valuable asset is their ability to earn an income. Unfortunately, there are risks that could affect your ability to earn income. For example:

- You may become ill, injured or disabled and unable to work

- You may lose your job and become unemployed

- When you retire your income from work stops.

In the case of any of these happening there will be consequences, not just for you, but also for any family members that rely on you to maintain a certain level of income.

RISKS ASSOCIATED WITH YOUR SPENDING AND BORROWING

These risks can arise for a number of reasons. You could be spending more than you are earning. This could be because you are simply not earning enough to meet the basic needs of you and your family. But, it could be because you want to buy things that give you the lifestyle that you aspire to but cannot afford.

When you overspend, for whatever reason, you may decide to take the risk of borrowing money to fund this spending. This can result in unaffordable interest payments leading to a growing level of debt (see the 'Borrowing' chapter).

RISK THAT YOU MIGHT LOSE ASSETS

If something you own is stolen or damaged it may need to be replaced, or maybe you damage something belonging to someone else and have to pay for the repairs. The more expensive the item, the greater the financial risk to you if it is damaged or stolen.

RISKS ASSOCIATED WITH INVESTING

To invest is to use your money to buy something that has the potential to grow in value. There is an element of risk with investments as there is no guarantee that what you have invested in will increase in value – in some cases it could even decrease in value, meaning you could lose money.

What people choose to invest in often depends on their attitude to risk. Some choose not to invest at all, some take very low risks and others may make a higher risk investment.

QUESTIONS

1. What could be the three most valuable assets someone might own in their lifetime?

2. Name three risks that could affect your ability to earn an income.

3. Explain how investing is different to saving.

CASE STUDY

Simone has met her friend Mei for a coffee. She is happy to order and get a table if Mei doesn't mind going to the cash machine for her to get some cash out. She gives Mei her debit card along with her PIN, which Mei puts into her phone notes so that she can remember it.

Over coffee, Mei tells Simone that she is planning to go on holiday soon and has seen a really great deal on an online travel agency. She has never heard of the agency, but the holiday is much cheaper than anywhere else she has seen it. While she has no savings at the moment, Mei is planning on getting herself a credit card to book the holiday.

Simone gives Mei the news that she has recently passed her driving test and is about to get a loan from the bank to buy a second hand car from a friend of a friend.

1. Identify the financial risks that Mei and Simone are taking.

2. Decide whether each risk is a low, medium or high-risk activity.

3. Discuss the implications of each risk and decide how Mei and Simone could minimise each one.

ACTIVITY

Different people have different attitudes to risk. Working with a partner, look at the 10 activities listed in the table below and rank them from 1 to 10.

1 = the activity you consider to be the least risky

10 = the activity you consider to be the most risky

As you rank them, discuss what risks might be related to each of them. When finished, compare your ranking order – are they the same? Why might there be differences of opinion?

ACTIVITY	YOUR RISK RANKING (1-10)	PARTNER'S RISK RANKING(1-10)
Crossing a very busy dual carriageway		
Sleepover at a friend's house		
Getting a lift in a friend's car		
Smoking cigarettes		
Going to watch a Premier League football match		
Playing games on a computer		
Watching TV		
Riding a bike without a crash helmet		
Sky diving		
Walking down a flight of stairs		

DID YOU KNOW?

If you are looking to borrow money the lender will assess the level of risk you present to them. Customers who are lower risk will often be able to borrow money at lower interest rates than those who are considered a higher risk.

 ACTIVITY

When will you have to assess the risk of financial decisions?

Draw a timeline from the age of 14 to 30. Place the following financial decisions on that timeline for when you think you might have to make them independently:

- Owning a car

- Choosing a savings account

- Paying for a holiday with friends

- Owning a pet

- Borrowing some money

- Starting to pay rent for accommodation.

Add two more of your own to the timeline.

INVESTMENTS

All investments have the potential to grow in value, but they can also decrease in value, meaning you begin to lose money. This is different to a savings account, where your money is protected, and grows according to the interest rate you receive.

Some common forms of investment include:

 ## SHARES

A share is a unit of ownership in a company; if you buy a share in a company then you own part of it. Companies raise the money that they need in order to operate and grow by selling shares. If a company performs well its share value will rise and any shares you have in that company will increase in value. You could then sell them at a profit. For example, you buy 100 shares at £1 per share therefore spending £100. After 3 years you decide to sell them all as they are now worth £2 per share, meaning that you will receive £200 for your 100 shares, making a profit of £100.

However, shares can also go down in value if a company does not do as well as expected and share prices can vary greatly from day to day. For example, the 100 shares that you bought at £1 per share are now valued at 80p per share, meaning that if you sold all of your shares you would only receive £80, making a loss of £20.

If you own shares you may also receive income from dividends, which are a portion of the company's profits paid out to shareholders.

This type of investment carries more risk than collective investments (see below) and is considered to be a longer-term investment.

More information on buying shares can be found in the 'Further your knowledge' section.

 ## COLLECTIVE INVESTMENTS

Many investors are not experts in investing. They may also be worried about taking a risk by investing too much of their money into one or just a few companies, which could perform badly and see their share price fall. One option is to invest in a unit trust which is run by people who are experts. These trusts may well invest in shares and commodities (such as property and gold) in order to spread the risk for an investor. The combination of the different areas of investment is known as the portfolio. Even if one area of the portfolio begins to fall in value, this may not impact the unit trust too much and may be balanced by growth in other areas of the portfolio. Even so it's important to realise that collective investments can still fall in value.

 ## PROPERTY AND OTHER COMMODITIES

Some people prefer to invest in actual products like gold and houses. As with shares, the value of these can go down as well as up. For example, you buy a house worth £100,000 but in 12 months the house is revalued at £98,000 meaning that you have lost £2,000 off the value of the property and the amount you paid for it. Five years later, the house is revalued again and is now worth £115,000, meaning that if you were to sell you could make £15,000 profit. One issue with these is that they can be difficult to sell quickly, so are not good if you might need your money in a hurry.

Bear in mind that some insurance policies also require you to pay an agreed amount of the cost of any damage if you make a claim – known as the excess. The insurer will then pay for anything more than this. Agreeing to a higher excess generally reduces premiums.

Self-insuring

Some people choose not to buy insurance if they consider the risk of something going wrong to be small. Self-insuring means having enough money saved, or saving an amount each month, which will be used to cover the loss of income or property if you lose your job, or covers the cost of replacing something you own if it breaks or is stolen.

DID YOU KNOW?

20% of all households in the UK have no buildings or contents insurance.

Source: media.shelter.org.uk October 2017

ACTIVITY

Andrei has recently bought a rescue dog called Casper from a local animal charity. Casper has been checked by a vet and he is fit and healthy to go to his new forever home with Andrei.

Andrei decides not to buy pet insurance, which costs £35 per month. Instead, Andrei will self-insure and pay for Casper's vet bills by saving £15 a month, which he thinks will cover the cost of any treatments Casper might need.

In the first year, Casper only requires his annual injections, costing Andrei £80.

1. What are the risks for Andrei by self-insuring?

2. By not choosing insurance, how much has Andrei saved over the first year?

3. How long would it have taken Andrei to save up for the annual injections?

4. In your opinion, was Andrei right to self-insure?

5. Think of three questions you should ask yourself before you decide to self-insure.

INSURANCE POLICIES

When taking out insurance you must make sure that it is the right policy for your circumstances, and that you will be covered if something were to go wrong.

As with any financial product, insurance policies will have full terms and conditions that detail what they will and won't pay out for and it is important to check these thoroughly to ensure that the policy is suitable for you.

Not all insurance is a good idea. Banks sold Payment Protection Insurance (PPI) alongside loans and credit cards for years, supposedly to cover repayments if you lost your job or were sick. And while not always a bad idea, it wasn't suitable for most people and was actually very expensive. So much so that over £30 billion has been repaid to customers in a huge mis-selling scandal.

Insurance companies often come up with new things that you can insure yourself against, even where the risk is minimal. So always examine the risk, work out whether you need the protection, or if you're protected in other ways (through other insurance you may already have), before signing up to new insurance policies.

DISCUSSION

Does it pay to be loyal?

Owen has been a loyal customer, automatically renewing his car insurance every year and never querying price increases. He believes that because he has insured his car with the same company every year, he will be getting the best deal.

Chris has just joined the same insurance company. His circumstances are identical to Owen's and they drive similar cars.

Who do you think gets the cheaper insurance? Explain your answer.

DID YOU KNOW?

Real Madrid Football Club insured Cristiano Ronaldo's legs for £90 million.
Source: www.telegraph.co.uk

ACTIVITY

Research other things that famous people have insured themselves for.

ACTIVITY

In pairs or small groups, draw three spidergrams – one each for a house, car and holiday. Try to work out the risks attached to each and write them onto the spidergram. When complete, consider these questions:

• What is the likelihood of them happening?

• How disastrous, upsetting or expensive might they be if they happened?

• Would you consider taking out insurance for any of these risks?

• Other than these three things, what else do you think you might have to take out insurance for?

CASE STUDY

Emil loves gadgets and always likes to have the latest technology for his phone and flat. He queued up to get the latest smartprhone and uses it all the time for photos, music streaming, maintaining his social media and staying in touch with his friends and family. He has the very best 4K UHD TV and the lighting and heating in his flat is voice controlled. He has fitted security cameras that can send an image to his smartphone if an intruder is detected. He cannot afford to buy and run a car but, as he lives in a town, he uses his e-bike a lot and now wants to upgrade it. He is considering taking out a loan to pay for the latest model.

Aliyah loves travelling and participating in adventure sports like mountain biking and white-water rafting. Originally from Sweden, she is also an accomplished skier and snowboarder. She rents a flat, but it is often empty whilst she travels. When she is travelling in the UK, Aliyah takes Rufus, her beloved 12-year-old collie, but when she goes abroad she pays friends to look after him. To get around in the UK, Aliyah has a 20-year-old campervan that she calls Hector.

Can you advise Emil and Aliyah on insurance? Recommend two types of insurance that you feel are important to Emil and two for Aliyah.

DID YOU KNOW?

The record pay-out by an insurance company in the UK to repair a car was in 2011 when the actor Rowan Atkinson (who plays Mr Bean) crashed his McLaren F1 into a hedge. It cost the insurance company £910,000. Mr Atkinson sold the car four years later for nearly £7.5 million more than he paid for it!

Source: www.mirror.co.uk

OTHER FORMS OF PROTECTION AGAINST FINANCIAL RISK

INDUSTRY REGULATORS

If you, as an individual, have a complaint about a financial business the first thing to do would be to talk to the business and give them a chance to put things right. If, after receiving their final response (usually within 8 weeks), you are still unhappy that would be the point to contact the **Financial Ombudsman Service.**

The Financial Ombudsman Service was set up by parliament to resolve individual complaints between financial businesses and their customers. They can look into problems involving most types of money matters – from payday loans to pensions, pet insurance to advice on buying shares. If they decide someone's been treated unfairly, they have legal powers to put things right.

The financial services industry is regulated by an independent body called the **Financial Conduct Authority (FCA)**. Any business or individual who wants to offer financial services to the public must be authorised by the FCA. If the FCA believes someone is misleading the public, for example, through false claims made in adverts, then it can investigate an organisation or individual, fine them and impose a ban on their activities.

The Gambling Commission was set up under the Gambling Act 2005 to regulate commercial gambling in Great Britain. Their objectives are to:

- Prevent gambling from being a source of crime or disorder, being associated with crime or disorder, or being used to support crime

- Ensure that gambling is conducted in a fair and open way

- Protect children and other vulnerable people from being harmed or exploited by gambling.

Like the FCA, they do not deal with individual complaints – they regulate the industry. If you had a complaint about a gambling business, you would talk to the business to try and get the problem resolved. If this did not work to your satisfaction you could then contact the **Independent Betting Adjudication Service (IBAS)**. IBAS was founded in 1998 and is a third-party organisation that settles disputes between gambling establishments registered with IBAS and their customers in the United Kingdom.

STATUTORY RIGHTS

In addition to the industry regulators, consumers are also protected by certain laws.

The Consumer Credit Act 2006 – This act gives protection to consumers when they are borrowing money. The Act lays down rules covering: the form and content of credit agreements and credit advertising, the method of calculating the Annual Percentage Rate (APR) of the total charge for credit and the procedures to be adopted in the event of default, termination or early settlement. This is also the Act that set up the Financial Ombudsman Service.

Advertising Standards Authority (ASA) – The ASA is the UK's independent regulator of advertising across all media. If you feel an advert about a particular financial service is misleading or incorrect you can complain to the ASA who will then investigate the matter.

Financial Services Compensation Scheme (FSCS) – This was set up in 2001 and is free to customers of UK registered financial institutions. It protects your money should anything happen to your bank, building society or credit union. The maximum amount is £85,000 per financial institution (or £170,000 for a joint account). So, let's say for example you have savings of £100,000 in a particular bank. That bank then gets into difficulties and eventually goes bust. Under the FSCS you are guaranteed to get £85,000 of your savings returned to you. As there is a maximum amount that can be compensated it makes sense for people with larger savings to spread them around so that they do not have too much money tied up in one particular organisation.

QUESTIONS

1. What is the role of the Financial Conduct Authority (FCA)?

2. If you had a complaint about a personal loan, who could you contact for help?

3. What is the purpose of the Gambling Commission?

4. What is the name of the organisation that regulates the media?

5. What is the total amount of savings that are protected under the Financial Services Compensation Scheme (FSCS)?

WHAT HAVE YOU LEARNT?

Using the knowledge you have learnt from the previous pages in this chapter, complete the activity and case study below:

ACTIVITY

Look at the following scenarios and decide a possible risk and reward for each.

SCENARIO	POSSIBLE RISK	POSSIBLE REWARD
Buying shares		
Playing games in an online casino		
Buying cryptocurrency		
Not taking out an insurance policy for a new phone		
Buying an antique watch		

CASE STUDY

Jodie works as an aerospace engineer testing aircraft. After her monthly expenses and putting some money into savings, she still has around £150 left at the end of each month.

Jodie does like to take calculated risks. She is not irresponsible and accepts that there are risks that come with looking for greater financial rewards. For example, Jodie only has car insurance, and for everything else she self-insures (puts money aside each month to cover anything unexpected).

She has never invested money before but is now considering her options and the balance between risk and reward that she is willing to take.

1. Is Jodie currently facing any possible financial risks?

2. Explain what Jodie means when she says she is "considering the balance between risk and reward".

3. Suggest some ways in which Jodie might chose to invest her £150, and explain the risks and rewards associated with each.

4. What would you do if you were in Jodie's position?

FURTHER
YOUR KNOWLEDGE

BUYING SHARES

When you buy shares in a company, you will usually pay tax. If you buy the shares online, you will pay Stamp Duty Reserve Tax (SDRT) and you will be charged 0.5% on top of what you have paid for the shares. For example, if you pay £2,000 for your shares, your SDRT payment will be £10.

If you buy shares through a stock transfer form (i.e. paper-based shares) you will pay SDRT charged at 0.5%, if the value of the shares you are buying is greater than £1,000. This is then rounded up to the nearest £5. For example, if you buy shares using a stock transfer form to the value of £2,995 you will pay £15 SDRT.

SELLING SHARES

If the profit you make when you sell your shares is greater than £11,700 (2018/19) in one financial year you will pay Capital Gains Tax, but only on any gain over this amount. If you are a basic rate taxpayer, you will pay 10% and if you are a higher rate taxpayer then you will pay 20%.

Look at the following scenarios and for each one:

a) Identify which tax the investor will pay

b) Calculate how much tax the investor will pay.

1. Danah purchases £11,800 of shares using the internet. After 3 years, Danah's shares are now worth £23,650 and she has decided to sell them. Danah is a basic rate taxpayer.

2. Emily pays £4,250 for some shares using a stock transfer form.

3. Juan paid £6,750 for his shares a year ago and they are now worth £8,320. He is planning to sell his shares and he is a higher rate taxpayer.

4. Oliver buys shares valued at £7,800 for £6,100 using an online bank.

INSURANCE

Joel has recently bought a new phone on contract costing him £60 per month for 2 years – the £60 includes a monthly payment for the phone itself, plus a monthly data, calls and texts package. The shop where he buys the phone from suggest that he considers taking out a mobile phone insurance policy, at an additional cost of £100 per year, with an excess payment of £100 if he loses or damages it.

Joel decides not to buy the insurance. A week after his purchase, disaster strikes, and he drops his phone and it no longer works. He takes it back to the shop where they discover that it is beyond repair and there is nothing they can do to fix it.

If he wants to replace his phone with the same model, it will set him back £1,000 just for the handset and, whatever he decides to do, he will still have to pay £60 a month for the original contract even though he no longer has the original phone – although he will be able to use the data, calls and texts with a new handset.

In pairs, answer the following questions:

1. If Joel had decided to purchase the insurance, how much would the phone and insurance have cost him for the 2-year contract?

2. Joel decides to replace his phone with the same model and learning from this mistake, he decides he will also take out mobile phone insurance to prevent any future possible damages or theft. How much has this whole experience cost him?

3. In your opinion, do you believe this insurance policy to be money well spent? Explain your reasons.

4. In the UK, approximately 82% of adults have a smartphone while only 20% of adults have mobile phone insurance.

   Why do you think this figure is so low?

(Source: http://www.assurantsolutions.co.uk/connected-insight/mobile-phone-insurance-insight-report-2015/)

INVESTING IN SHARES

Sandeep and Noor decide to risk some of their savings on the stock market, buying shares in a variety of different UK companies to try to make a profit on their investments. They track their investments weekly using the London Stock Exchange website to see how they are performing in the table below:

COMPANY NAME	NO. OF SHARES OWNED BY SANDEEP AND NOOR	PRICE BOUGHT PER SHARE (IN P)	VALUE OF INVESTMENT (£)	PRICE TODAY (IN P)	TODAY'S VALUE OF INVESTMENT (£)
The Blue Company	2500	6p		7p	
YellowSquare	48	725p		722p	
Green Edit PLC	150	140p		139p	
Red-Champ	500	58p		56p	
TOTAL					

1. Create an investment tracker for Sandeep and Noor like the above example.

2. Which company shares are most profitable? And by how much?

3. How much profit or loss have Sandeep and Noor made in total from when they purchased the shares?

4. If the price of YellowSquare shares falls by 10% and the price of Green Edit PLC shares increase by 15%. What is the value of their investment portfolio now?

5. What risks are involved when investing in shares?

6. Imagine you have £1,000 to invest in shares. Undertake your own virtual share challenge; choose some companies on the London Stock Exchange and track your shares once a week for 4 weeks and see how much you could have made (or not!).

SECURITY AND FRAUD
WHY SHOULD I KEEP INFORMATION ABOUT MYSELF SECURE?

In this chapter you will explore what is meant by identity theft and fraud.

You will see how identity theft can happen and how information about your identity may be fraudulently used by people who are trying to make money by breaking the law. You will also discover what to do if someone steals your identity, plus look at some of the ways you can protect yourself against identity theft.

 DID YOU KNOW?

In the UK in 2017;
- **Almost 175,000 case of identity fraud were recorded**
- **Nearly 25,000 victims of fraud were under the age of 30**
- **84% of identity frauds were committed online**
- **The biggest percentage increase in victims of fraud were under 21.**

Source: Cifas

WHAT IS FRAUD?

Fraud involves a person dishonestly and deliberately deceiving a victim for personal gain of property or money. In the UK, the first laws on fraud were set out in the First Statute of Westminster in 1275. So, fraud is not a new offence but methods of committing it have greatly evolved in recent times with the rise of new technology. In particular, the internet has provided increased opportunities for fraudsters to commit crime on a very large scale.

What is identity theft?

Identity theft is one common type of fraud; it is the act of a person illegally obtaining information about someone else. Thieves might try to find out the following types of personal information: full name, maiden name (the original surname of a person if they decided to change it when they got married), address, date of birth, National Insurance number, phone number, email address, passwords, bank details and debit or credit card numbers.

Identity theft is not a new crime; here are some historic examples:

The book of Genesis in the Bible tells the story of Jacob and Esau, which is considered by many to be the first documented act of identity theft. Jacob posed as his older brother Esau in the hope of tricking his dying father into believing he was the older son so that he would inherit his father's estate when he died.

In 1925, Victor Lustig posed as the deputy director general of the Ministry of Posts and Telegraphs in Paris. He met with a group of scrap dealers and offered them the chance to buy the Eiffel Tower. One of the scrap dealers fell for the con and Lustig escaped with their money. He was eventually caught and sentenced to 20 years in Alcatraz (a notorious American prison).

In 2006, the UK government became so concerned about the rise in identity theft that it announced plans for everyone in the UK to carry an ID card. However, these plans were scrapped in 2010 following concerns about the cost of the scheme and how effective it would be. There were also worries over how much personal data would be collected, how it would be stored and how it would be used.

During the American Wild West era, in the late 19th century, outlaws would murder people to acquire a new name and life story. This false identity helped the outlaws to stay one step ahead of the law.

In the 1960s, Frank Abagnale Jr. assumed a number of identities, including an aircraft pilot and a doctor. Before he reached his 19th birthday he obtained more than $2 million through fraud. Aged 21, he was sentenced to 12 years in a federal prison for multiple counts of forgery. His story was made into a 2002 film called Catch Me If You Can starring Leonardo DiCaprio and Tom Hanks.

QUESTIONS?

1. What type of personal information could be taken during identify theft?

2. Why has the internet increased the risk of identity theft?

3. What could fraudsters do with the identities they take?

WHAT ARE THE DIFFERENT METHODS USED TO CARRY OUT IDENTITY THEFT?

Physical

Bank card skimming – This usually occurs when someone, for example a shop assistant or waiter, gets your information by "skimming" or copying your debit or credit card information when you make a purchase. They often then sell the information to professional criminal gangs. This can also be done when a special storage device is attached to an ATM or cash machine. The device reads the magnetic strip on your card which thieves use to commit fraud.

Bank card scanning – This is when a fraudster uses a card-reading machine or mobile app to scan the details of your contactless bank card without you even knowing. Using Near Field Communication (NFC) technology, the fraudster only has to be within a few inches of where you keep your bank card or credit card in order to scan your details. Once they have your details they can use them to carry out contactless purchases – you might only know when you see some strange purchases on your bank statement.

Theft – Stealing a purse or wallet used to be the main way of obtaining personal information. Although fraudsters now often use the internet for identity theft, many people carry a lot of personal details in their purse or wallet, so this is still a widely used method of getting information in order to steal identities.

Bin raiding – Fraudsters pay people to go through the rubbish that an individual throws out. They are looking for bank and credit card statements, tax details, insurance documents, gas, electricity and telephone bills, personal letters and any other pieces of personal information that can help to steal an identity.

Changing your address – Thieves divert your post to another location by completing a change of address form. They can then read all your bank statements and other financial information. If they cannot divert your mail, thieves may simply steal it – especially when your post box is separate from your house/flat.

Digital

Hacking – Hacking occurs when criminals successfully guess or decipher your passwords, security questions, and/or Personal Identification Numbers (PINs). They can then access any accounts you have. Many hackers use social networking sites like Facebook to get information about you that can be used to answer security questions. Some hackers will break into a company website and steal the company identity. This means you could order goods from a website that you think is genuine, but they simply take your money and you never hear from them again.

Malware – This term is short for malicious software. It is designed specifically to make its way onto your device i.e. your desktop, smartphone, or tablet and to manipulate and/or damage them. In addition, malware can also record and steal your personal information such as bank account details. There are many different types of malware: viruses, worms, trojans, bots, spyware, adware, and ransomware.

Malware gets onto your device in a variety of ways:

- On software installed from a website

- From a spam email

- Using a flash USB drive already infected with malware

- Clicking on pop-up windows.

You can protect your computer by installing a firewall to prevent unauthorised access, and antivirus software which can prevent, detect and remove malware.

Social

Phishing – By pretending to be financial institutions or companies, thieves can send fake emails or pop-up messages to get you to reveal your personal information. You should never click on links in pop-up windows or in spam/junk e-mail and should avoid responding to such emails.

Vishing (voice phishing) or phone scams – These typically involve fraudsters deceiving people into believing they are speaking to a member of bank staff or a representative of another trusted company or agency, such as a government department. Usually, the fraudster will convince the person that they have been a victim of fraud and will ask for personal and financial information to gain access to their account. An identity thief could also phone someone to inform them that they have won a prize, but in order for them to receive it they would need to give some personal information; this is then used for the thief's benefit.

Smishing (SMS phishing) – This is when someone tries to trick you into giving them your private information via a text or SMS message. Many people tend to be more inclined to trust a text message than an email and people are less aware of the security risks involved with clicking on links in text messages. A common tactic used by a smisher is to say you must take immediate action – for example, if you don't click on a link and enter your personal information then you're going to be charged per day for use of a service.

ACTIVITY

Use the information on the 10 different methods used to carry out identity theft (physical, digital and social) to draw a two-column table with method of fraud in column one and how to prevent the fraud in column two.

In pairs or groups, complete the table by adding at least two tactics to stop the intentions of the fraudsters. The first one has been done for you in the example below:

METHOD OF FRAUD	TACTICS TO STOP THE FRAUD
Bank card skimming	Don't let anyone take your card away to make a purchase. Always cover your hand when putting your PIN into an ATM to withdraw cash.
Bank card scanning	

DID YOU KNOW?

Since November 2016, Royal Mail have successfully intercepted and stopped three million scam mail items from reaching UK homes.

Source: Royal Mail

Last Collection Time
Monday to Friday
4.45pm

ACTIVITY

How well do you know your terminology?

Here are seven methods used by fraudsters to get personal information from your computer. Can you match the definition to the key terms below?

1. A piece of code or software program which is capable of reproducing itself. Often used to damage a computer by corrupting the system or destroying or modifying data and files.

2. A type of malware often disguised as legitimate software, which is used to gain access to a computer in order to watch what the user is doing without them knowing, steal sensitive data or take over the system remotely.

3. An application that performs an automated task, used maliciously these can gather passwords, email addresses and financial information from computers.

4. Acts like a virus but uses a network connection to spread itself to multiple computers.

5. Software that is installed on a user's computer, often without their knowledge, and can monitor activity.

6. Software that automatically displays or downloads material, such as banners or pop-ups when a user is online. The software often tracks and records users' personal information and internet browsing habits.

7. A type of malware that prevents or limits users from accessing their system, either by locking the system's screen or by locking the users' files unless some money is paid.

Key Terms: adware, bots, ransomware, spyware, trojan, virus, worm.

CYBER CRIME

It's not just individuals who are targeted by fraudsters, according to the government's 2018 Cyber Security Breaches Survey nearly half the businesses in the UK fell victim to cyberattacks or security breaches in 2017. Most businesses rely on digital communications or services and store vast amounts of personal data (e.g. names, email address and bank details) about their staff and customers.

Scammers can hack into customer databases to send fraudulent emails and pretend to be the organisation online or use viruses or malware to corrupt files and systems.

If you are informed that your personal details have been lost or stolen by a company who holds your data, you should change the password of the email account associated with the company straightaway and keep an eye on your bank account for any suspicious activity.

ACTIVITY

Read the three emails below. Do you think any of them might be scams? List anything you think might be suspicious.

Email 1

From: Alejandro and Pedro Lopez Giveaway Team <jasgt24@giveaway.com>

Subject: **Congratulations – you have won £1 million**

Hi

As you may well remember from the national news earlier this year Alejandro and Pedro Lopez won £50 million on the EuroMillions lottery. However, they decided this was far too much for them to spend and decided to give away £1 million to each of six random people around the UK. Your email was one of the ones selected!!

Alejandro and Pedro do not want any publicity from this so please do not try to contact them. We will transfer your money into your account once you have completed the attached bank details form and returned it to ourselves.

We look forward to receiving your form and well done!

Best wishes from us all

The Alejandro & Pedro Lopez Giveaway Team

Email 2

From: info@donate.eu.com

Subject: **dear friend**

Dear frend

We are from a small vilage in nigeria that was affected by the recent sunami that you seen in the news. Our busness is lost and we are homless.

Since we have lost all our relatives and children we have to send this letter and APPEEL FOR DONATIONS.

We will be very greatfull for any money you can send to help us get our busness started again.

This letter is being sent to lots of people in the hope that we get help to get food. The United Nations help a bit but not much.

We prey to God and Allah that you will help us. Please click on this link to send your bank detales with a little donation sunami-appeal.com

Thank you

Email 3

From: Windows Live Team <mail.check@netscape.com>

Subject: **Storage limit reached – act now!**

Dear User

Courtesy notice from the admin team

You have reached the storage limit for your mailbox on the database server

You will be blocked from sending or receiving new messages if your email is not verified within 48 hours

Please click BELOW to verify and access e-mail restore

CLICK HERE

Thanks

WINDOWS LIVE TEAM

TIPS FOR SPOTTING A FAKE EMAIL

- The sender name or email does not look valid. Sometimes the name looks genuine but when you check the actual email address it's something completely different.

- Are there spelling, punctuation and grammar mistakes?

- Look at how the email begins – is the email addressed to you or is it a general greeting?

- Look at the signature. Lack of details about the sender or how you can contact a company strongly suggests a phish. Legitimate businesses always provide contact details.

- If something looks too good to be true it probably is!

Take another look at the three emails in the last activity. Is there anything you missed earlier?

QUESTIONS?

1. How do you check the full email address from a sender, and what type of things would make you think the sender could be fake?

2. Name three methods of social identify theft.

3. What is the difference between digital and physical identify theft?

ONLINE FRAUD

Lots of people shop online so it's no surprise that this is a growing area of opportunity for identity theft. Creating fake websites or selling fake goods online are just two of the ways you can be fooled into sharing your personal and financial details with fraudsters.

It's not only fake goods that people can be duped into buying, potential renters can be tricked into paying an upfront fee for a property that doesn't exist. In these instances, fraudsters will advertise a property online. The advert will look genuine and often include photos and contact details. The advertiser will then ask the potential tenant to pay an upfront fee so that no one else can rent it, often before they have viewed the property in person, but in reality the property won't exist or will have been "rented" to multiple people. Victims then lose the fee that they have paid and won't be able to rent the property they think they have secured.

Reports of rental fraud increase in the summer months, indicating that fraudsters are targeting people looking for holiday rentals, and students searching for accommodation before term starts in September.

DID YOU KNOW?

Cybercrime is any criminal act dealing with computers and networks, including traditional crimes conducted through the internet. Victims of cybercrime lost £28 million between October 2017 and March 2018.

Source: Action Fraud

 CASE STUDY

Jess wanted to buy a special piece of jewellery with the money she received for her 16th birthday. She found a necklace she liked; it was quite expensive at £170 but she knew the brand and that it was supposed to be high quality.

She thought she would be buying it direct from the maker's website. It was very professional with no spelling or grammar mistakes and, as the name of the site had UK in it, she assumed they were based in the UK.

However, the fraudsters involved had committed identity theft, stealing the identity of the genuine website.

Jess's mum placed the order using her credit card and the site said it would take between 7-10 working days for the order to arrive. After about 5 days of waiting, the credit card bill arrived, and Jess's mum was shocked to see that the necklace seemed to be coming from China.

After three weeks, she rang the credit card company and told them that she had received nothing from the website, not even a confirmation email. They told her to wait 30 days and then they would send a form to fill out that would ensure she'd get her money back. She was incredibly relieved that she paid with a credit card – it is standard practice that purchases over £100 are covered, otherwise they would have lost the £170.

What could Jess and her mum have done to avoid this fraud?

ACTIVITY

How to protect yourself against online shopping or auction fraud

Read the following tips and then use the words below to fill in the gaps:

1. When making online payments, only pay for items using a secure payment service – look for a URL starting with "https" and a closed _____ symbol, or a payment provider such as _____ which helps to protect you.

2. Check the website address. A tactic often used by fraudsters is to change the address very _____ (e.g. if they're spoofing an eBay site they may have an address such as "…@ebayz.co.uk" whereas the real site is "…@ebay.co.uk").

3. When using retail websites, find out exactly who you are dealing with. If it is a _____ company, you are in a much better position to sort out the problem if something goes wrong.

4. Browse the website. Take a couple of minutes to double-check the site. Maybe visit the homepage or the "About us" pages and read the text there. Watch out for poor _____, such as spelling and grammar mistakes, or phrases that don't sound quite right. Any company offering goods or services should list a place of business, as well as a _____ or email address through which to contact them. If none of this information is available, you should treat the website as suspicious.

5. Make sure you read the _____ on the website or seller. This will give you useful information about recent transactions other buyers have made. Look at reviews across a number of sources, such as Trustpilot, Feefo or Sitejabber, which aggregate customer reviews.

6. Check the item's _____ carefully – ask the seller questions if you're not sure of something.

7. Be extremely careful when buying things from people with little or no selling _____.

Missing words: description, English, feedback, history, padlock, PayPal, phone number, slightly, UK

DID YOU KNOW?

If you have spent over £100 and up to £30,000 on a credit card and become a victim of identity fraud, the Consumer Credit Act 1974 means you should be able to claim that money back because your credit card issuer is jointly liable with the retailer that you are paying the money to if something goes wrong.

WHAT HAPPENS IF SOMEONE STEALS YOUR IDENTITY

If fraudsters gain direct access to your bank account or credit cards, they may leave you with no funds to pay for everyday living costs which can cause short term financial stress. The more serious and complex the identity fraud the longer it can take to recover any stolen funds, which can cause more long term financial difficulties.

Identity fraud can also affect your credit history. If a fraudster uses existing credit that you have (e.g. a credit card) or applies for new credit in your name this could leave evidence of debt or missed payments on your credit report. It is possible to correct this information, but it can take a while to sort out and to demonstrate to your credit provider that you have been the victim of crime. Even a temporary drop in your credit score may make it harder for you to borrow money – a big problem if you are in the middle of opening a new bank account, buying a car or applying for a mortgage. Refer back to the 'Borrowing' chapter for definitions of credit history, credit reference agency, credit report and credit score.

Although it is certainly possible for a victim to recoup stolen funds and to clear their name of any wrongdoing, the emotional toll of identity theft can last far longer than any financial worries. Victims can blame themselves for their identity being stolen and feel more vulnerable to it happening again.

CASE STUDY

Dev and his partner Lena have both been victims of identity theft in the last three years. They told their neighbours about this, and it turned out that several people who live in the same building have also been victims. All their letterboxes are on the street outside, so it is easy for thieves to access their mail, including bills and bank statements.

When a thief gets hold of a bill or bank statement they then have enough details to be able to apply for credit accounts (e.g. credit cards or shopping accounts) and then steal the cards or account detail.

Dev only knew that this had happened to him when he received a statement showing that he owed a credit card company over £2,500. He didn't have an account with this provider, but the thief had been able to take one out in his name and spend thousands of pounds that he was now being billed for. He had no idea what else they might have done with his personal details; they could have signed up to websites or even applied for a passport.

He contacted the credit card provider who helped him get the money back, but he found the whole experience very worrying.

What could Dev, Lena and their neighbours have done to avoid having their identities stolen?

HOW TO PROTECT YOURSELF FROM IDENTITY THEFT

 ## 10 TOP TIPS

1. Never share passwords or PINs with others.

2. Use strong passwords and PINs – don't use family names; include a mix of upper and lower-case letters, numbers and symbols. Aim for a minimum of 8 characters in a password.

3. Do not use the same password or PIN for more than one account.

4. Shred or burn any unwanted financial documents – do not put them straight into recycling.

5. Make sure your computer has up to date firewall, anti-virus and anti-spyware programs. Up to 80% of online threats can be removed by doing this.

6. Try to limit the amount of personal information that you carry around on a day-to-day basis.

7. Limit the amount of personal information that you give away on social networking sites. Remember, your real friends already know where you live and when your birthday is! Be alert – think what information about you can be gained by pictures of your first car, new driving licence or when you are holidaying away from home.

8. Make use of any security settings offered by social media platforms and mobiles. Examples of these include privacy settings, captcha puzzles and warning pages informing you that you are being redirected offsite.

9. Only accept online friend requests from people who are familiar.

10. Always review your bank account statements (and credit card statements when you get one). You should promptly compare receipts with account statements, whether it is on paper, mobile or online. Watch for transactions you don't recognise, especially very small amounts – these could be the sign that someone has your details.

 ## SOCIAL MEDIA PRIVACY SETTINGS

Social media use is on the increase in the UK (over 50% of the population are expected to be on Facebook in the coming years). Users commonly post their full name, home town and date of birth on Facebook and that's an awful lot of personal information that could be accessed by fraudsters! Facebook allows users to control their privacy settings to limit who can see what is being posted. Have you checked your settings recently?

 ## QUESTIONS?

Read the 10 ways to protect yourself from identity theft and answer these questions:

- Which do you think are the three most effective ways to protect your information?

- Compare your top three to your friends or classmates – do you agree or not?

- If you had to choose one of these to act on tonight, which one would it be?

ACTIVITY

Here are the top 10 worst passwords of 2016, as published in SplashData's "Worst Password List". In no particular order they are:

football, qwerty, password, princess, 1234, 12345, 123456, 1234567, 12345678, 1234567890

Which do you think is the worst?
What three rules would you put in place to ensure you had a more secure password?

PASSWORD TOP TIPS!

1. Look again at numbers 1-3 in the "how to protect yourself from identity theft" list.

2. Do not use the name of your pet, family member, school, favourite team, or anything that somebody could easily guess.

3. Always log off if you leave your device and anyone is around. It only takes a moment for someone to steal or change the password.

4. Avoid entering passwords on computers you don't control (like computers at an internet cafe or library) – they may have malware that steals your passwords.

5. Avoid entering passwords when using unsecured Wi-Fi connections, like at the airport or in a coffee shop. Hackers can intercept your passwords and data over this unsecured connection.

6. Consider using a password manager (sometimes called a password safe or vault). This is typically a software application or a hardware device that is used to store and manage a person's passwords. Typically, all stored passwords are encrypted, requiring the user to create a master password to access all managed passwords. There are a number of password managers available for your use – some paid for, some free of charge.

7. Be careful not to enter passwords over "open" Wi-Fi networks. These networks are much more susceptible to hacking attacks.

SECURITY QUESTIONS

As well as requiring you to enter your password, many websites now also ask a security question as an extra check to verify your identity, something financial institutions have been doing since the early 20th century. Websites often ask you to choose from a standard set of questions, commonly including, "What is your mother's maiden name?", "What was the name of the first street you lived on?" or "What was your first pet called?". When choosing from a given list of security questions, pick the one which would be most difficult for someone else to find out your answer to.

Some websites will let you set your own question, in which case make sure you set it as something that a fraudster would not be able to guess or work out from information they know about you already or could easily find out.

A good security question will have the following characteristics:

- It will be easy for you to remember, even 5-10 years from now

- It will have thousands of possible answers so can't be guessed, even by friends or family

- It's not a question you would have discussed on social media, so the answer can't be searched for

- Has a simple one or two-word answer

- It never changes.

BIOMETRIC VERIFICATION

Biometric verification is a way of verifying someone's identity by recognising one or more distinguishing and unique biological features, including fingerprints, hand geometry, earlobe geometry, retina and iris patterns, and voice waves.

This technology is still being developed but many mobile phones and computers now use fingerprints, iris patterns, and voice recognition in order to control access to the device and specific apps.

TWO-FACTOR AUTHENTICATION

Many websites now add an extra layer of security in order to confirm the user's identity. They will ask for your username and password as normal, but on top of that they might text a verification code to your mobile phone, send an email with a code or web link or, often in the case of online banking, provide you with a physical security device like a card reader which uses your card details and PIN to randomly generate a unique passcode to authorise log in and certain transactions.

By asking for two (or more) forms of verification, it makes it harder for fraudsters to gain access to your devices and online accounts, because knowing the password alone is not enough to pass the authentication check.

WHAT SHOULD YOU DO IF YOUR IDENTITY IS STOLEN?

The first thing to do is ACT FAST if you think you have been a victim of identity theft. Contact your bank or credit card company and alert them to your suspicions. Their contact details can usually be found on the back of your debit/credit card or on any communications you have received from them such as monthly statements.

If you have fallen victim to identity fraud you should contact Action Fraud who will advise you on what to do. If you receive some communication which makes you think you have (e.g. mail that seems suspicious or implies you have an account with the sender which you don't) don't ignore it. You can also contact Action Fraud for advice if you believe that someone has stolen your identity.

If you are over 18 you can get a copy of your credit report, which is one of the first places you can spot if someone is misusing your personal information, even before you have suffered a financial loss. Review every entry on your credit report and if you see an account or even a credit search from a company that you do not recognise, notify the credit reference agency.

You may need to contact all the financial organisations that you deal with, if the fraudster has reached them they may be able to help you get your money back and, if they haven't been affected, they may be able to put security measures in place to stop any fraud or theft from any accounts you hold with them.

If you have information about those who are committing identity crime you can tell the independent charity Crimestoppers, which you can do anonymously.

HELP AVAILABLE IF YOU ARE A VICTIM OF IDENTITY THEFT

- **Your bank or building society** – Most now have specialist units that deal with identity theft.

- **Citizens Advice** – If you feel that your bank or building society are not meeting their obligations to you in relation to the identity theft, you may want to talk to someone at your local branch of Citizens Advice.

- **Victim Support** – This charity provides help and advice to people who have fallen victim to a wide range of different crimes, including those who have experienced identity theft/identity fraud.

Be aware that you need to exercise the same caution if you are using a Victim Support forum as you would if you were using any other type of internet forum. Although it is sad to say, some fraudsters actually visit these forums as they are aware that the users may be particularly vulnerable or more likely to share their personal information.

DID YOU KNOW?

There are over 100 types of fraud listed on the Action Fraud website.

ACTIVITY

Go to the Action Fraud website and find out about one type of fraud that you don't already know about. Explain what it is to your friends/classmates.

DISCUSSION

Identity theft is one type of fraud, but there are also many others. A few examples include: charity donation fraud, holiday fraud, lottery fraud, mobile phone fraud and romance fraud. Details of all of these can be found on the Action Fraud website.

Discuss with a partner or in a small group if there are any that could affect you.

 CASE STUDY

Surfed Arts

In 2017, Action Fraud, working with the City of London Police and in partnership with Get Safe Online and the Society of Ticket Agents and Retailers (STAR), set up a fake ticketing website to show just how easy it is to be tricked into buying fake tickets online.

How the "sale" worked

A series of ads were shown on Facebook to advertise "Surfed Arts", the fake ticket sales website.

The website was made to look like a secondary ticket provider, imitating the way fraudsters offer fake tickets online. The Facebook ads targeted people living in areas where bands or artists were due to play sell-out concerts.

Adverts were shown to fans of Adele in London, Ed Sheeran in Manchester, Iron Maiden in Birmingham, Coldplay in Cardiff and Bruno Mars in Leeds.

Fans who clicked through were taken to the Surfed Arts website where they were immediately told that they were not able to buy tickets and advised on how to protect themselves from falling victim to real ticket fraudsters in the future.

How many people tried to buy tickets?

More than 1,500 people tried to buy tickets from the fake ticket sales website set up to raise awareness of ticket fraud.

Why set up the website?

More than 21,000 people have reported falling victim to ticket fraud in the last 3 years.

More than £17 million has been reported to be lost to ticket fraudsters in the last 3 years.

Victims are most likely to be men in their twenties.

Source: www.actionfraud.police.uk

How can you avoid falling victim to ticket fraud?

MONEY MULES

A money mule is a person who transfers illegally gained money on behalf of others, usually through their bank account. Criminals contact people who are often in need of money through job adverts on social media, just like the one below.

NEED MONEY NOW?

Earn from the comfort of your own home.

Make £200 per week and no experience necessary.

TEXT NOW ON 0790150958

How it works:

- You sign up to a fantastic job opportunity and provide your new employer (the criminal) with your bank account details. More often than not you will not be aware that you are about to be involved in illegal activities

- Once they have gained your trust, the criminal transfers money to your bank account

- Once the money has cleared your bank account you will be told the details of a different bank account to transfer the money to

- You will be told how much you can keep as your "fee".

Once the criminals have your bank account details they will keep encouraging you to transfer more. By this point you will be aware of the scam/fraud that is taking place and you will probably try to get out of the agreement. This might be difficult as they can often threaten you.

Banks have systems in place to identify suspicious movement of money and if you are caught illegally transferring criminal funds, it is likely that your bank account will be closed and you may find it hard to get credit and/or loans in the future. Worst of all, this can carry a prison sentence of up to 14 years.

 ACTIVITY

1. In your opinion, do you believe the advert to be a genuine job advert? If so, why? If not, why not? Explain your answer.

2. If you thought that the advert wasn't genuine, who would you inform about your concerns?

3. Using all of your knowledge of security and fraud, design a factsheet for young people about how they can identify and avoid money mule schemes.

 DID YOU KNOW?

Almost 9,000 young people in the UK aged between 18 and 24 were caught acting as money mules in 2017.

Source: NatWest Moneysense

WHAT HAVE
YOU LEARNT?

Using the knowledge you have learnt from the previous pages in this chapter, complete the activity and case study below:

ACTIVITY

Write a blog post aimed at alerting young people to identity theft and/or fraud.

To help you to complete this task look at the following short videos which can be found on YouTube:

- Data to Go (Cifas)
- The Devil's in Your Details online (Action Fraud)
- The Devil's in Your Details phone (Action Fraud)
- Digital Safety TV ads (Barclays)

If you are unsure where to begin, type "How to write a blog post" in your search engine – you will find plenty of advice on the internet.

CASE STUDY

Noah receives the following text:

WEBANK4U_FRAUDDEPT

Customer, please contact us immediately using the link below. We have reason to bel you're account has been accessed without your consent.

The Fraud Team

www.webank4u/ frauddept.com

In a panic, Noah clicks through using the link provided and immediately enters his customer number and PIN. Within seconds he receives another message…

> Thankyou for your details. We will cll you shortly
> The Fraud Team

Still thinking about it, he looks again at the messages and starts to wonder if they are genuine. He checks his online banking app and, to his horror, he realises that all of his savings have gone.

1. What method of identify fraud is this?

2. Looking back at the text, Noah has spotted a number of concerns. Identify three details that indicate that the text is not genuine.

3. How could Noah have protected himself against this identity fraud?

4. List five things Noah should do now.

FURTHER
YOUR KNOWLEDGE

PERSONAL DATA

In 2017 Ofcom asked 1,800 adults how confident they were about knowing how to manage access to their personal data online. By this, Ofcom meant whether these adults knew how to stop companies from getting access to their personal details, for example, their date of birth, address, phone number, etc. The chart below shows the answers that were given as percentages.

■ Very confident　■ Fairly confident　■ Neither/Don't know　■ Not very confident　■ Not at all confident

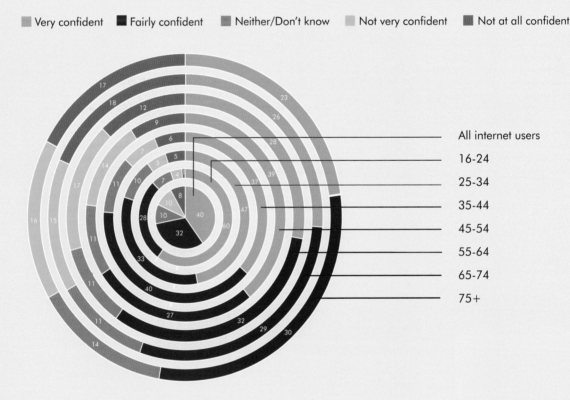

Source: www.ofcom.org.uk

1. What percentage of all internet users were either very or fairly confident about managing their data online?

2.　**a)** Which age groups were more confident than this?

　　b) Why do you think this is?

3.　**a)** Which age group was the least confident about managing their data online?

　　b) Is this the response that you would have expected? Explain your answer.

4. Ofcom have provided you with the raw data, showing the actual number of males and females who responded to this question. Calculate these as percentages and draw a bar chart representing this information like the one to the left.

	TOTAL	VERY CONFIDENT	FAIRLY CONFIDENT	NEITHER/ DON'T KNOW	NOT VERY CONFIDENT	NOT AT ALL CONFIDENT
Males	900	392	288	80	80	60
Females	900	333	288	99	99	81

5. Finally, write a paragraph summarising the key outcomes of this data.

CHECKS MADE

The infographic below shows the checks people make when purchasing online before entering financial information.

 67%
If the site looks secure (padlock symbol or https)

 56%
If I'm familiar with the company or brand

53%
If there is a link to another reputable service like Paypal

 33%
If there is a guarantee my details won't be shared with anyone else

 24%
If the site is recommended by friends/family

 70% Mentioned at least one of the five above

 15%
If the site is listed by a search engine such as Google or Bing

 11%
If it's the only way to get the service or product I want

 5%
I enter my details whenever they are required

 24% Mentioned at least one of the three above

 1%
Don't know

Source: www.ofcom.org.uk

6. In pairs, write a summary explaining the key points of this data. In your opinion, is there anything about the data that you were surprised about?

GENERAL DATA PROTECTION REGULATION (GDPR)

The General Data Protection Regulation (GDPR) came into force in May 2018 and is used to protect consumer data and ensure data is securely stored, making businesses think about the data that they collect, why they need it and how they use it.

All UK organisations, as well as EU or worldwide companies that hold UK customer data, must follow these regulations. The key points of GDPR are:

- All customers must give their consent to using their personal data
- All customers have the right to obtain confirmation of whether their personal data is being used and how
- All customers have the right to ask organisations to delete their personal data and stop it from being distributed
- All customers are entitled to receive an electronic report for free about the data that is kept by a business.

Carry out some research into GDPR and test your knowledge below:

1. GDPR is designed to protect and control the use of your personal data, but what personal data does this cover?

   a) Just my name, address and date of birth

   b) The above plus medical records, social network data and bank details

   c) Anything that you believe is "personal data" to you

2. You decide to quit a social media app, what must the social media company do?

   a) They must tell you how you can order them to delete all of the personal data that they hold about you

   b) They are under no obligation to delete any of your data

   c) They ask you to complete an online questionnaire about why you want to leave

3. You have a fall at work and when you get to hospital you are unconscious and require an operation. What is your GP allowed to disclose about your medical history?

   a) Only information about previous medical conditions

   b) Nothing until you gain consciousness

   c) Anything that will help save your life

4. If there is a breach in the security of your data, what does the company affected have to do?

   a) Nothing, they don't have to do anything

   b) Call the police

   c) Inform the authorities within 72 hours of it happening

5. Once a business has your personal information, how can they use it?

   a) Whichever way they want

   b) They can sell it to other companies

   c) They can only use it in the way that was explained to you before you gave them consent to use it

YOUR MONEY MATTERS
GLOSSARY

Account

Arrangement with a bank or building society to hold your money in an account and to take it out when you need it.

Advertising Standards Authority (ASA)

The UK's independent regulator of advertising across all media.

Annual Equivalent Rate (AER)

Takes into account the charges and the interest paid on savings and shows it as an overall percentage rate. Used as a way of comparing different savings products; the higher the AER, the better the return on your savings.

Alternative credit

Credit arrangements outside the mainstream, which usually end up being extremely costly.

Annually

Something that is done every year.

Annual Percentage Rate (APR)

The total cost of a loan, taking into account the interest you pay, any other charges and when the payments are due. Used as a way of comparing different borrowing products; the higher the APR, the more expensive the loan.

Apprenticeship

An apprenticeship combines practical training in a paid job with study.

Asset

Something a person owns that has a monetary value (e.g. property, investments, cash).

ATM (Automated Teller Machine)

Also known as a "cash machine" or "hole in the wall", this is an electronic machine that dispenses cash and other banking services using a cash withdrawal card and a PIN (Personal Identification Number).

Automatic enrolment

All workers between the age of 22 and retirement are automatically enrolled in a workplace pension.

Bb

BACS (Bankers Automated Clearing System)

A fast service that allows transfers of money to be made electronically from one bank to another (e.g. salaries).

Bad debt

Debt that does not provide ongoing benefit or a financial return to the borrower.

Balance

The amount of money you have in your account at any particular time or that you owe on your credit or store card, or on a purchase after the deposit has been paid. It will be shown on your statement.

Balance transfer

Allows you to take out a new card to pay off debt on old credit and store cards that are charging interest. The new card may have 0% interest or have a lower interest rate than you are currently paying, so you will become debt free quicker as the payments you make reduce the debt, rather than paying off the interest.

Bank

A financial institution owned by its shareholders. It aims to maximise profits for the shareholders through its financial activities. It must lend money in order to stimulate economic growth, and, in turn, profit. To lend money, a bank must take a certain amount of deposits, which it does in the form of current and savings accounts opened by individuals and businesses.

Bank account

A service from a bank or building society which lets you pay in money, get cash out and pay bills, etc. The bank keeps a record of all transactions.

Bank loan

Money that you borrow from your bank and then pay back with a pre-arranged interest rate.

Bank of England

The UK's central bank responsible for setting the base interest rate in order to try and keep the economy stable. This base rate can influence the rates offered to savers and borrowers for some financial products.

Bank statement

A piece of paper or online document that shows all the money that has been paid into an account and paid out from an account. Statements are usually sent each month.

Banking apps

Many UK banks have apps that allow you to manage your accounts with them, and transfer money to people or businesses.

Bankruptcy

A court order given when someone cannot pay the debts they owe. An official receiver takes control of your money and property, and deals with creditors.

Bank card skimming

The act of "skimming" or copying your debit or credit card information when you make a purchase.

Bank card scanning

Use of a card-reading machine or mobile app to perform fraud by scanning the details of your contactless bank card without you knowing.

Base rate

Interest rate set by the Bank of England, which other financial institutions (such as banks) use for guidance when setting their rates.

Basic Rate Tax

The basic rate of Income Tax is 20%. Most tax payers will pay 20% tax on any income above the personal allowance.

Benefits

A government system that provides financial support to people who are eligible for it (e.g. state pension, universal credit).

Bill

Statement that shows how much money is owed for something (e.g. gas, electricity, phone).

Bin raiding

When thieves search through household rubbish looking for personal information that can be used to carry out fraud.

Biometric payments

Payments for goods made using finger scanning technology or facial recognition systems.

Biometric verification

A way of verifying someone's identity by recognising one or more distinguishing and unique biological features.

Bonds

A fixed income investment where an investor loans money to government or public company at a fixed rate of interest for a specified period of time.

Bonus

Payment made to an employee in addition to their basic salary, often for working hard or hitting targets.

Borrowing

Getting money from somewhere that you intend to pay back. You might borrow informally from friends and family or take out a formal loan, with a written agreement, from a bank or building society.

Budgeting

The process of managing your money and the balance between your income and your outgoings.

Building society

An organisation that is owned by its members, some or whom will be customers saving or borrowing from the society. They often offer a range of financial services and are similar to banks.

Buildings insurance

Type of insurance policy that pays out if the structure of your home is damaged (e.g. your house is damaged by fire).

Bursary

Cash award given to a student by a college or university towards the cost of their studies.

Business expenses

The costs incurred when you run a business (e.g. utilities, company vehicles, office equipment).

Business income

Money a business earns from its customers by selling products and services.

Business rates

Rates charged by local councils on most non-domestic properties (e.g. shops, offices, restaurants).

Cc

Capital

The amount of money you originally have, save or invest, before any interest or other return or loss is taken into account. It could also be an amount of money that you have borrowed.

Capital Gains Tax

The tax paid on profits from selling investments such as shares if their value is over a certain amount.

Cash ISA

A long-term tax free savings account.

Catalogue

A printed magazine/book that showcases goods for sale. You can buy them on credit and pay in weekly or monthly instalments, usually with added interest payments. The goods will usually be delivered by post.

Charges

Fees and interest that you have to pay, for example, when you borrow money or buy on credit.

Cheque

Paper-based payment method used for buying goods, paying bills and given as gifts.

Collective investments

A form of investing where an investors money is pooled into a much larger fund and managed by a fund manager to invest in a range of assets. This aims to spread the risk associated with investing.

Commission

A payment based on the value of sales made. Sometimes this will be in addition to a basic salary.

Commodities

Something that can be traded, bought, or sold.

Compound interest

The usual type of interest paid on savings and loans, based on the principal plus the interest already paid so far (i.e. interest on interest), so the savings or the loan will grow by increasing amounts (unless money is taken out or the loan paid off).

Consumer

Someone who buys something.

Consumer Credit Act 2006

This act gives protection to consumers when they are borrowing money.

Consumer rights

Consumer rights protect you when you buy goods and services. These are rights by law (including the Consumer Rights Act 2015), which a shop or service provider can't change.

Consumer society

A society in which people place a high value on possessions and in which they are encouraged to buy more.

Contactless payment

A way of making a payment by tapping or waving your contactless device (e.g. credit card, debit card, smartphone) on or near a contactless reader.

Corporation tax

A tax on profits and capital gains made by companies, calculated before dividends are paid.

Council tax

Tax paid to the local council for local services such as libraries, police, waste collection, etc.

Credit

An account "in credit" means that there is money in it that is available to be spent. If you obtain goods or services "on credit" it means that someone (for example, a bank or credit institution) has given you the money as a loan to make the purchase.

Creditor

An individual or company that is owed money.

Credit cards

A small plastic card available to 18 year olds and older from most banks, which allows you to borrow money up to a certain limit. When you buy something with your credit card, the amount you spend is added to your total borrowing. Every month you are sent a statement to show how much you have borrowed and how much you need to repay. If you don't repay the full amount, you will start paying interest.

Credit history

A record of loans you have taken out or credit card payments made or missed. This information is stored by credit reference agencies, which supply details of your credit score/rating to financial institutions when you take out further loans.

Credit limit

The maximum amount the store card or credit company will lend you at any time.

Credit rating

An estimate of how risky it would be to lend a person or an organisation money based on their credit history/record.

Credit reference agency

An agency that holds information on adults. This information includes public records (e.g. electoral register entries) and credit history information. They make this information available to lenders when you apply for credit, who then use the information to decide whether or not to offer you credit.

Credit report

A detailed report of an individual's credit history, current credit arrangements, address history and details of anyone you are financially linked with.

Credit score

A score given by a credit agency based on your credit history, personal and financial circumstances. It reflects the level of risk in lending to you and the likelihood of you paying credit back and helps them to decide whether you are likely to repay the loan you are asking for.

Credit union

A community-focused, non-profit-making organisation that encourages saving and lends money to members at low interest rates. To use a credit union you have to become a member.

Cryptocurrency

Virtual or digital currency produced by a public network, rather than any government, that uses cryptography to make sure payments are sent and received safely. It can be used to buy products and services but is generally not accepted in shops.

Currency

Money in any form used to buy goods and services e.g. euro, pound, dollar. Different countries use different currencies.

Current account

An account which helps you to manage your day-to-day money – pay bills, receive incoming money and keep money secure.

Cybercrime

Any criminal act committed through the internet using computers and networks.

Cyber security

Technology, processes and controls that are designed to protect systems, networks and data from cybercrime.

Dd

Debit

Money taken out of an account is "debited" from that account.

Debit card

A small plastic card used to buy things in a shop or online without using cash or a cheque. When you make a payment or withdraw cash with your debit card, the money is taken straight out of your account electronically, if you have the money available to spend. You cannot borrow money on a debit card.

Debt

Money you owe to another person or organisation.

Deductions

Amounts taken from your gross pay directly by your employer (e.g. Income Tax, National Insurance contributions, pension contributions, student loan).

Default

To default on a loan means to fail to make payments that are due.

Degree

A higher education qualification.

Delayed gratification

Postponing the sense of enjoyment from immediate spending to sometime further into the future.

Deposit

Money paid into an account. Can also mean an initial payment that secures the purchase of something, normally a percentage of the total amount.

Digital footprint

Information about a person that exists on the internet as a result of their online activity.

Digital wallet

An app that allows you to store all your credit, debit and customer loyalty card details on your phone.

Direct debit

An instruction to your bank to release money from your account to pay bills and other amounts automatically. The billing company has control and requests the money from the bank directly, and can change the amount requested.

Discount

Money which is taken off the price of something. You may need to collect coupons or vouchers before claiming the discount. Sometimes shops and businesses give a discount to their employees.

Disposable income

The amount of money left at the end of each month once all your bills have been paid.

Dividend

Money from a company's profits paid to people who have shares in the company.

Early repayment charge

A penalty or fee for repaying a loan before the end of the term.

Easy access account

An account that allows you to withdraw money at any time without prior warning.

Economy

The state of a country or region in terms of its production and sale of goods and services, and the way its government manages its money.

Electronic transfer

A way of moving money from your account to another.

Employee

Someone who is paid to work for an organisation, company or an individual.

Employer

Organisation, company or individual who pays someone else to work for them.

Estimate

An educated guess.

Excess

Some insurance policies require you to pay an agreed amount of the cost of any damage if you make a claim. The insurer will then pay for anything more than this.

Exchange rate

The exchange rate tells you how much you get when exchanging one currency for another (e.g. 1 British pound might be worth 1.5 US dollars).

Excise duties

A type of tax charged on goods produced within the country.

Expenditure

The amount of money you spend on goods or services.

Expenses

Things you need to spend money on in order to live (e.g. rent, bills, food).

Fair trade

The fair-trade movement aims to make sure that workers and producers get paid fairly.

Fee

A sum of money you pay, for example, to have a loan or credit arranged for you. Or a one-off payment that is paid or charged for a professional service.

Financial adviser

A person or company who can assess your financial needs and give you advice about money and suitable financial products. Some advisers can also manage investments for you. An independent financial adviser (IFA) is one that doesn't work for a specific bank or other seller of financial products, and can, in theory, offer a wider range of options.

Financial Conduct Authority (FCA)

The independent body that regulates the financial services industry.

Financial exclusion

Lack of access to mainstream banking and other financial services.

Financial Ombudsman Service (FOS)

Set up by parliament to resolve individual complaints between financial businesses and their customers.

Financial risk

To gain financial rewards, there is often some element of risk involved – the outcome of a financial decision may not be certain or guaranteed.

Financial Services Compensation Scheme (FSCS)

The scheme that protects your money should anything happen to your registered bank, building society or credit union.

Financial situation

Your financial situation refers to how much money you receive in wages and/or benefits and how much money you have saved up. It also includes how much money you owe and any financial arrangements you have made for the future, such as a pension. Sometimes people will also ask you about your regular outgoings, such as the amount you pay in rent.

Fixed interest rate

An interest rate guaranteed to stay the same for an agreed period, regardless of whether the lender changes their rates.

Fixed rate savings account

Your saved money is "locked away" for a specified period of time.

Fraud

When a person dishonestly and deliberately deceives a victim for personal gain of property or money.

Fraudster

A person who commits fraud.

Full time

Usually working 35 hours or more a week, full-time workers are usually provided with a contract of employment and receive benefits such as holiday pay, sick pay and pension opportunities.

Gambling

Betting money, which can result in either a win or a loss – for example, through playing the lottery, fruit machines or casino games.

Gambling Commission

Set up under the Gambling Act 2005 to regulate commercial gambling in Great Britain.

General Data Protection Regulation (GDPR)

Regulations in force to protect consumer data and ensure data is securely stored; making businesses think about the data they collect, why they need it and how they use it.

Gig economy

A term used to describe the growing trend towards short-term contracts compared to permanent employment.

Good debt

Debt that provides an ongoing benefit to the borrower or will result in some kind of financial return.

Graduate training scheme

A work-based training programme that allows recent graduates to gain practical experience with a company.

Grant

Cash award usually given for a very specific purpose, like studying abroad or undertaking a research project.

Gross

A total amount of money before any deductions, such as tax or National Insurance.

Gross income/pay

The total income you receive before anything is taken away from it such as Income Tax and National Insurance contributions. Gross pay will always be bigger than net pay.

Gross interest

Interest on savings before any tax is taken off.

Hh

Hacking

When criminals successfully guess or decipher passwords, security questions, and/or PINs (Personal Identification Numbers).

Health insurance

Insurance which covers medical expenses if you are ill. It may also provide a regular income to you if you are too ill to work.

High cost credit

Forms of borrowing which attract excessively high interest rates e.g. payday loans, unarranged overdrafts, and can even be illegal and unregulated e.g. borrowing from loan sharks.

Higher Tax Rate

The higher rate of Income Tax is 40%.

Hire purchase (HP)

A way of paying for goods if you don't have all the money up front (often used for cars). An initial deposit is usually paid, followed by a series of regular payments to cover the balance and any interest over a fixed amount of time, the same as repaying a loan. You would not own the car until you have completed the hire purchase agreement.

Home buildings insurance

Insurance which covers the cost of repairs to the structure of your home in case of damage.

Home contents insurance

Insurance which covers your possessions in the home against loss or damage.

Hourly rate

Being paid a set amount for every hour you work.

HM Revenue and Customs (HMRC)

The government department responsible for tax collection and benefit payments.

Ii

Identity theft

This is a type of fraud and is the act of a person illegally obtaining information about someone else often for financial gain.

Income

Money that comes to you through earnings, gifts, selling things you own, from your parents, etc.

Income protection

A type of insurance that guarantees you some income if for any reason you are unable to work.

Income tax

A tax payable on almost all types of income, at various rates depending on the level of income.

Independent Betting Adjudication Service (IBAS).

Founded in 1998, IBAS is a third-party organisation that settles disputes between registered gambling establishments and their customers in the UK.

Inflation

A continual increase in the general level of prices. This means that over time a given amount of money will buy fewer goods and services.

Inheritance

The passing on of money or assets when someone dies. It can also include gifts given while the person is still alive.

Instalments

Weekly or monthly repayments made to pay off a loan or goods bought on credit.

Instant access account

A savings account where you can get your money back without having to give any notice. They generally attract lower rates of interest than accounts where notice is required.

Insurance

A way to protect yourself against the financial loss of something going wrong. Insurance provides a guarantee of compensation for specified loss, damage, illness, or death, in return for payment of a specified premium.

Insurance premiums

Money you pay to the insurance company, either annually or monthly, for the insurance.

Insurance policy

A contract from an insurance company telling you what you are covered for, and how much money the company is prepared to pay out.

Interest

The reward you get for keeping your money with a bank or a building society. It is also the cost you pay when you borrow money through a loan or credit agreement.

Interest rate

This is the percentage that is paid on savings or charged on loans.

Invest

To use money to buy something that may increase in value over time, for example, jewellery, property or shares in a company.

Investment

Products that have the potential to grow in value, but they can also decrease in value, meaning you begin to lose money.

ISA (Individual Savings Account)

An account where you don't pay tax on interest earned. There is a set limit of how much you can save in an ISA each tax year.

Jj

Junior ISA

A long-term, tax-free savings account for children under 18, contributed to by the UK government, which becomes a normal ISA when they turn 18.

Ll

Life expectancy

The average period that a person may expect to live.

Life insurance

An insurance that pays money on your death, or in some cases if you become critically ill while you are covered. Life insurance is often taken out to cover a mortgage, so that if you die during the mortgage term the loan will be paid off.

Lifetime ISA

A long-term, tax-free savings account, contributed to by the UK government, that is often used for first-time property buyers or to build savings for when you retire.

Loan

A sum of money that you borrow from a person or organisation, usually with interest.

Loan cover

Insurance that will protect you if you cannot repay a loan due to illness, unemployment, etc.

Loan shark

Someone who lends money without being regulated to do so. As they are not regulated there is no limit to the interest rate they charge or the penalties they can apply.

London Stock Exchange

The main stock exchange of the UK where shares, bonds, etc. are sold.

Lottery

A form of gambling that involves the drawing of numbers for a prize (e.g. the National Lottery).

Lump sum

A one-off payment.

Mm

Manageable debt

Debt taken on that the borrower can afford to repay.

Maintenance loans

A loan to cover your day-to-day living costs, like accommodation, food, transport, phone and laptop costs when at university. The maximum you can borrow depends on how much your parents/guardians earn. Maintenance loans are paid directly to you at the start of each term, and not paid back until you have finished the course and are earning above a certain amount.

Malware

Short for malicious software, designed specifically to make its way onto your device i.e. your desktop, smartphone, or tablet and to manipulate and/or damage it.

Minimum repayment

The minimum amount you must pay off each month on the debt you have on credit or store card payments.

Money mule

A person who transfers illegally gained money on behalf of others, usually through their bank account.

Mortgage

A type of secured long-term loan used to buy a property. If you do not keep up the mortgage repayments the mortgage provider (often a bank) can repossess your property.

Motor insurance (third party)

Legally required insurance which will cover your costs if you damage someone else or their property (i.e. a third party).

Motor insurance (third party, fire and theft)

Insurance which also covers the policyholder's own vehicle if it is stolen or catches fire.

Motor insurance (fully comprehensive)

Insurance which covers the cost of damage to yourself and your own vehicle, as well as any damage you may cause to someone else or their property.

Nn

National budget

The annual budget for the UK set by HM Treasury.

National Insurance contributions

A government deduction from your wages used to pay for benefits that you might need to claim, and your state pension when you retire. A plastic card with your NI code is sent to all UK residents just before their 16th birthdays. Employers and employees both pay contributions.

National Minimum Wage

The minimum pay per hour that most workers under the age of 25 are entitled to by law. The rate will depend on a worker's age and if they are an apprentice.

National Living Wage

The minimum pay per hour most workers aged 25 and over are entitled to by law.

Needs

These are the absolute necessities; the things you really cannot do without.

Net

Indicates a sum of money from which certain deductions have already been taken away (e.g. tax).

Net income/pay

Your net income/pay is the total you earn in a week, month or year after any deductions have been made. Sometimes called take-home pay.

Notice accounts

An account where advance warning usually has to be given if you wish to withdraw money from it without being penalised.

Occupation

Your job, work or profession (e.g. bricklayer, checkout operator, teacher).

Outgoings

Your expenditure (e.g. rent/mortgage, bill payments, savings).

Overdraft (arranged)

A way of borrowing money through your current account. Arranged overdrafts are set in advance and you can spend money up to the agreed overdraft amount.

Overdraft (unarranged)

If you go overdrawn without asking the bank in advance or have an arranged overdraft and spend more than the amount agreed, this is an unarranged overdraft. This is likely to incur penalties and can be very costly.

Overtime

Time worked in addition to normal or contracted working hours. Can be paid or unpaid.

P45

A document that an employer has to provide when you leave a job so that the right amount of tax can be deducted from your earnings.

P60

A summary of your pay and the tax that's been deducted in the tax year. Your employer should give you a P60 to keep as a record at the end of every tax year.

Part time

Working fewer hours than full time but receiving the same treatment and benefits (though these may be proportionate to the number of hours worked per week).

Password

A word or phrase only you know that is used to prove your identity to access online accounts.

PAYE (Pay As You Earn)

When deductions are collected from an employer before the individual is paid their salary/wages.

Payday lender

Lenders who provide very short-term loans on relatively small amounts of money.

Payments

Money you pay out, for example, on your rent or mortgage, on materials you need for your business, interest on loans, money for utilities such as gas and electricity.

PayPal

An electronic payments system that allows you to make secure payments to an individual or to purchase items online.

Pension

An income paid regularly by the government or a private company to a person who does not work anymore because they have reached retirement age.

Pension contribution

The amounts you and your employer pay into your pension, usually calculated as a percentage of your basic salary and taken from your gross pay.

Pension scheme

A type of savings plan to help you save money for later life, unlike normal savings you cannot use your money until you reach retirement age.

Personal details

Information about an individual that can be used to identify them (e.g. name, date of birth, address).

Personal loan

When money is borrowed for a non-specified purpose and generally paid back in monthly instalments.

Personal Savings Allowance

The amount of interest that can be earned on savings before tax has to be paid on it.

Personal Tax Allowance

The amount of income you don't have to pay tax on.

Pet insurance

Insurance that will cover vet fees if your pet needs an operation or other medical treatment.

Phishing

A method used by fraudsters to try and gather personal information using deceptive emails and websites.

PIN (Personal Identification Number)

A four-digit security number used with cash machine, credit cards and debit cards. It is like an electronic signature that stops anyone else using your account.

Piecework

Payment for each item produced. The more items produced the more pay received.

Policyholder

The person (or people) named on an insurance policy.

Portfolio

A range of investments held by a person or organisation.

Premium bond

A form of savings account offered by the government-backed savings bank – National Savings and Investment (NS&I).

Price comparison websites

Websites that have been developed specifically to compare the prices of goods from a range of suppliers and retailers.

Principal

The original amount of savings deposited, or debt taken out.

Private sector

The part of a country's economy that is controlled by private individuals, businesses or groups.

Profit

The amount of money left after all costs and expenses have been deducted from income.

Public sector

The part of a country's economy that is controlled or supported financially by the government.

Rr

Regular saver account

A regular sum of money must be added to the account each month.

Rent

Money paid to the owner of the property where you are living.

Rental fraud

A type of fraud where potential tenants are tricked into paying an upfront fee to rent a property which either does not exist, has already been rented out, or has been rented to multiple victims at the same time.

Repayment mortgage

A repayment mortgage is a property loan, where regular payments pay off both the interest and a proportion of the original loan.

Repayments

The sums of money you pay back weekly or monthly on your loan or credit.

Repossession

When a mortgage lender takes back ownership of a property when a borrower is unable to afford their mortgage repayments.

Retirement

The period in a person's life when they stop working and start receiving a pension. Those with a private pension may be able to retire earlier if their pension fund is large enough.

Return

The amount you get back when you invest money.

Rights

The protection that is given to you by law; for example, you have a right to compensation if your bank goes bust and you lose money.

Risk

Another name for chance or uncertainty e.g. the risk that you may become unemployed, or the risk that you do not have savings.

Ss

Salary

An amount of money paid to an employee for a job, usually paid directly into his or her bank account every month.

Saving

The act of putting money aside for future use. Saving can also mean reducing the amount you spend.

Savings

The amount or value of the money you put aside for future use.

Savings accounts

Accounts specifically designed for you to save money in, usually best for saving larger amounts.

Scholarship

Cash award given to a student who does particularly well in their exams preceding university or college. The scholarship may be awarded by the university or a company and may pay the tuition fees for a course in full or in part.

Second hand

Items which are not new and have been owned by someone else.

Secured loan

A secured loan requires something that gives the lender security in case you cannot pay the loan back.

Security question

An extra level of security used to verify your identity when accessing online accounts, only you should know the answer to the question.

Self-assessment

The way in which self-employed people calculate and pay their Income Tax.

Self-employed

A person is self-employed if they run a business for themselves and take responsibility for its successes and failures.

Self-insuring

Not taking out an insurance policy but having enough money saved, or saving an amount each month, which will be used to cover the loss of income or property if you lose your job or covers the cost of replacing something you own if it breaks or is stolen.

Shareholders

People who invest money in a company by buying shares in it, hence owning part of it.

Shares

A unit of ownership in a company.

Sharia banking

A way of banking following Islamic laws about money; for example, profit and loss is to be shared, interest is not given or taken etc.

Short-term contract

This can be on a full or part-time basis but is only for a fixed period of time.

Shift payment

When you are paid for working unusual hours, for example, working during the night, in addition to normal pay.

Simple interest

A quick and easy method of calculating the amount of interest payable between any two dates.

Small print

A product's terms and conditions, typically written in small letters and should be read carefully.

Smishing (SMS phishing)

A type of fraud where someone tries to trick you into giving them personal or financial information via a text or SMS message.

Stamp Duty Reserve Tax

A tax applied when you buy shares.

Standard of living

The quality of life enjoyed by an individual or household.

Standing order

A method of paying regular amounts from your bank account automatically. You are in control and instruct your bank to pay the money to a particular person or company. It's your responsibility to change the payment (e.g. the date or amount) if it needs to be changed.

Statement

A document from the bank or building society that shows all your recent payments into, and withdrawals from, your account. You should check it with your own records.

State pension

A pension paid by the government and to qualify for it you must have paid National Insurance contributions for a certain number of years.

Stocks and Shares ISA

Investing in a range of shares, bonds and funds without paying tax on the dividends paid out.

Store cards

Store cards are like credit cards but are available from shops rather than banks. They can only be used to buy things at particular shops. Anything you spend on your store card is borrowed money. If you do not pay off the full amount each month you will start paying interest on it.

Student Loans Company (SLC)

Non-profit making government-owned organisation that provides loans and grants to students in universities and colleges in the UK.

Tt

Take-home pay

Your actual monthly salary after deductions such as Income Tax and National Insurance contributions (i.e. net pay).

Tax

A fee charged by a government on a product (VAT), income (Income Tax), or activity (road tax) to finance government expenditure on public goods and services, such as the police, the NHS, street lighting or street cleaning.

Tax allowance

The amount of money you can earn before paying income tax.

Tax code

Shows how much income you can earn before you start to pay Income Tax – your tax allowance. It is the first four numbers of your tax allowance followed by a letter.

Tax year

A 12-month period running from 6th April one year to 5th April the next year. Taxes, such as Income Tax, are worked out over this period.

Taxable income

The amount of income used to calculate how much tax an individual or a company owes to the government in a given tax year.

Term

The time for which something lasts (e.g. how long you have to pay back a loan).

Terms and Conditions (T&Cs)

Often called "the small print" and are the set of rules surrounding a financial product.

Total deductions

The total amount that will be taken from your gross pay and will be shown on your payslip. What's left after this is your take-home pay.

Tracker mortgage

This tracks or moves in line with a declared interest rate (usually the Bank of England base rate).

Transaction

Any payment in or out of a bank account.

Travel insurance

Insurance which covers loss of luggage, travel cancellations or disruptions, or if you have to pay medical expenses because you fall ill on holiday, etc.

Tuition fees

The amount charged by universities to students to pay for the cost of the course.

Tuition fee loan

A loan which covers the full cost of your university course. This is paid directly to the course provider, and not paid back until you have finished the course and are earning above a certain amount.

Two-factor authentication

An extra layer of security in order to confirm your identity to access online accounts. On top of a password and security question, this could be texting a verification code to your mobile phone or sending an email with a code or web link.

Uu

UK Voluntary Living Wage Rate

Set by the Living Wage Foundation campaign group, this is independently calculated and designed to reflect the "real cost of living in the UK and London". It tends to be higher than the National Living Wage but is not enforceable by law.

Unit price

The price for one item or measurement, such as a pound, kilogram, or pint, which can be used to compare the same type of goods sold in varying weights and amounts.

Universal Credit

A payment to help with living costs which you might be able to get it if you're on a low income or out of work.

Unmanageable debt

Debt that is taken on with no means to repay it.

Unsecured loan

An unsecured loan does not involve security for the lender, but as they are taking a greater risk the APR (Annual Percentage Rate) tends to be higher.

Utilities

Services such as gas, electricity and water.

Utility bills

Bills with charges for electricity, water, gas and telephone.

University

A higher education institution where students study for degrees and academic research is done.

Vv

VAT (Value Added Tax)

A tax paid by the consumer for goods and services.

Variable rate interest

When the interest rate you are charged is not fixed, so interest payments may change if the lender changes their rate.

Vishing (voice phishing)

A type of fraud where someone tries to trick you into giving them personal or financial information over the phone.

Wages

The amount you are paid on a weekly or monthly basis.

Wants

These are the items, services or experiences you would like to buy if you had the money to do so.

Withdrawal

Money taken out of your account.

Workplace pensions

These are set up by your employer, and a percentage of your income will be paid into the pension. This is taken off your gross income before it is taxed so your pension contribution is tax free.

Zz

Zero hours contracts

Casual contracts that offer no guarantee of any work.